DON ASLETT'S OFFICE

Here's a formula that
with those piles of pa
pair of scissors, a stap
marker or Sharpie, ta
and paper for notes (s

OUT!

Label your first box **OUT**. This is an easy one, because much of that stuff that's been lying around all this time is defunct or defiled or outdated. A giant chunk of it is now gone in only the time it takes you to glance at it quickly, confirm that it's true clutter, and cast it.

ROUTE!

Label the second box **ROUTE.** Into this second box goes the worthwhile stuff that belongs somewhere else or to someone else. Toss all this into the Route box and when you're done, pick up that whole boxful and put or send everything back where it belongs.

DOUBT!

The third box should be labeled **DOUBT.** You might still want or need it, but you're not 100 percent sure what it is, or you want to check on it further. The unbendable rule of this box is that you work on it every single day until all the doubts are resolved and it's E-M-P-T-Y, right down to the bare cardboard.

SPROUT!

Label the last box **SPROUT**. Into it goes the good business-related stuff you really wanted and are ready to use at last. This is the high-grade ore, the notes and ideas that could change the world (or at least your job or company). Whatever you do, remember you really have to activate or file this stuff now, not just re-pile it!

THINGS TO REMEMBER

WHERE AND HOW YOU STORE things is important.

GET IT OFF THE FLOOR. Always store things up on either a skid or pallet or blocks or some 4 x 4s—anything to get the bottom away from contact with the floor.

REPACKAGE IT to protect better and to make it more useful, findable, and stackable.

GO FOR FIRST-CLASS CONTAINERS. Make sure it's sturdy if you want it to hold up in storage.

MARK ALL SIDES of each container with the contents. If you find the one you think you want at the bottom of a thirteen-foot stack, you can find out what's in it without renting a forklift.

MAKE DEJUNKING EASY. A nice big waste container in your storage area will help it stay clean.

LIGHT: always have plenty of it in storage areas. It encourages neatness.

The Office Clutter Cure

2nd Edition

The Office Clutter Cure

2nd Edition

Get Organized, Get Results!

Don Aslett

America's #1 Cleaning Expert

Adams Media
Avon, Massachusetts

Published by
Adams Media, an F+W Publications Company
57 Littlefield Street, Avon, MA 02322. U.S.A.
www.adamsmedia.com

ISBN: 1-59337-332-5

Printed in Canada.

J   I   H   G   F   E   D   C   B   A

Library of Congress Cataloging-in-Publication Data
Aslett, Don
The office clutter cure / by Don Aslett.—2nd ed.
p.   cm.
Includes index.
ISBN 1-59337-332-5
1. Paperwork (Office practice)—Management. 2. Office management. I. Title.
HF5547.15.A85 2005
651.5—dc22
2005009561

This publication is designed to provide accurate and authoritative information with regard to the subject matter covered. It is sold with the understanding
that the publisher is not engaged in rendering legal, accounting, or other professional advice. If legal advice or other expert assistance is required, the services
of a competent professional person should be sought.

—From a *Declaration of Principles* jointly adopted by a
Committee of the American Bar Association and a
Committee of Publishers and Associations

Many of the designations used by manufacturers and sellers to distinguish their prod-
ucts are claimed as trademarks. Where those designations appear in this book and Adams
Media was aware of a trademark claim, the designations have been printed with initial
capital letters.

Interior cartoon illustrations by jimhunt.us
Interior technical illustrations by Michelle Dorenkamp
Interior layout and design by Electronic Publishing Service, Inc. (TN)

This book is available at quantity discounts for bulk purchases.
For information, call 1-800-872-5627.

Contents

77   Chapter 5
Now for That Big Bad Backlog (of Paper) . . .

89   Chapter 6
Those All-Too-Cluttered "Common Areas"

103   Chapter 7
The Clutter You Can't See . . . Mental Clutter

115   **Chapter 8**
Ducking the Deluge:
Preventing Future Clutter

133   **Chapter 9**
Clean Desk Secrets

163   Chapter 10
Overcoming Fear of Filing

177   Chapter 11
Desk for Success: Design Clutter Out

Acknowledgments

When you clean offices for a living, you gain a lot of insight and information just working your way through tons of good old office clutter every night. I've furnished and run many an office myself, too, over the years in my many different businesses, and worked closely with many other professionals who work out of offices.

For the second edition of this book, once again, I didn't have just the benefit of my own more than forty-five years of frontline exposure to the office environment. I collected input from office inhabitants all over the country—I had them tell me where the pressure points were, what was wrong, in their own words. Thanks for all your "bits," big and little—this book and hopefully the workplace world is much better for them. A special thank you to the following office clutter elves: Dave Hermansen, Susan Waddell, Jenny Behymer, Jeannette Washburn, Dana Zimmerman, Martha Jacob, and Oscar Collier; as well as to Adams Media—Gary Krebs, Paula Munier, and Bridget Brace; and to my general manager Tobi Flynn and my editor (and still head pack rat) Carol Cartaino.

Introduction

I clean offices for a living—I may even clean yours, if it happens to be among the 400,000,000 square feet of office space my nationwide cleaning company, Varsity Contractors, services each night. Believe me, the act of cleaning up after people day after day gives insights you won't find in any library!

I've shared the secrets of the professional cleaners in more than a dozen books now, starting with *Is There Life After Housework?* way back in 1981. From my travels and writing, and from my own experience cleaning tens of thousands of homes and offices, I can say with confidence that clutter is responsible for at least 40 percent of the time we spend on "upkeep"—cleaning and maintenance. Almost half of all our time, energy, and money goes just to tending and shuffling junk and clutter. Having helped you all dejunk at home with books like *Clutter's Last Stand, 2nd Edition*, it is now time for you to go after all the clutter in that other place you spend so much time—the OFFICE.

If you're among the 99.9 percent of us who have a "career clutter" crisis brewing, I think you'll find this book helpful. Hopefully, it will inspire and enable you to finally achieve the impossible dream of an orderly office.

You have nothing to lose but a few hundred pounds of junk, and that feeling of hopelessness you've had for too long!

How It All Began

It didn't take us humans long to learn that we needed special locations to do some things—to eat, to sleep, and to groom ourselves, for instance. Soon, we had official places to perform all kinds of different duties.

The more people dealt with one another, the more they found themselves bartering, trading, selling, shipping, and yes, even warring and stealing. There was soon a need for a place to make plans, tally up deals and transactions, fill orders, keep records, reorder designer fig leaves, and leave messages. And so the office was instituted!

From Papyrus to Pulp: Let's Put It on Paper

Eventually we needed a more convenient way to record all this. So we began our investigation into what would turn out to be one of the most important materials ever made, something that to this day we've never quite gotten control of: paper.

Once we started using it, we couldn't live without it, and so one of the all-time greatest ingredients of office clutter was born.

And shortly, a place without provision for all this processing was inconceivable. We might as well have some comfort and convenience if so much time was going to be spent doing "paperwork." And so the first office furniture was boldly introduced. Someone conceived a tablelike contraption to provide additional room to write and read maps. And even in these dark early days it was discovered that "working late at the office" was an ironclad excuse for almost any neglect elsewhere.

Then Came Bureaucracy . . .

We expanded, along with our paper clutter, into ever larger companies, banks, local, state, and federal government, the U.S. Mail, and created other faster and more complicated ways of getting things from one place to another. Railroads came, and the West was won, which meant ever more records and documents and a need to keep track of them. In this era, some new office additions became either necessary or stylish, such as safes, strongboxes, and the big one: files!

Proof-establishing and rear-end-covering were important now, so "a bookkeeper" was a new office necessity. (And believe it or not, all bookkeeping was done in one large tally book.)

Where There Was a Wall . . .

There was a way to display prowess in the office. Long before the Roaring Twenties, people had discovered that an office could "roar" for them. It wasn't just a place for paper processing, but for prestige, politics, pettiness. The workplace didn't have to be a workhouse. You could show up and show off at the same time.

Getting an "office job" became the aspiration of American workers everywhere. Offices became bigger, better, and more beautiful. Office machine inventors worked night and day to automate the office. Office supply people came in platoons, one right after another. Gadgets not even God had thought of were created. The electric cords for all this snaked under and around desks and everywhere.

Coffeepots, plants, and copiers, and eventually computers, fax machines, and more gadgets, became permanent parts of the office scene, too.

Which Brings Us Right up to Today . . .

And what to do about *this* . . . this book will tell you how and why to do it.

In these pages you'll learn how to clean up your workspace, and why it's one of the most important things you can do for yourself and your career.

Chapter 1

Is It Really That Bad?

The Growth of Offices . . .

and Office Clutter

Most of us have at least one office or workspace somewhere, and many of us have two or three—at our job, at home, at school, at the club, at church, even in our car! Ninety-five percent of these areas are suffering the many painful symptoms of too much. The more that comes in, the less seems to go out. The more organizers we get, the less organized we are. The more fashion, the less function.

For over a half century now I've watched office obesity develop into a full-blown, crippling disease. As our office clutter mounts, we're ever more intimidated and frustrated by it. We engineer drainage and removal of water and liquid wastes from society to prevent hazardous buildup, but the paper and electronic files that pour into our offices are never flushed out.

We've become masters of accumulation and failures at eradication. We have a serious case of office constipation.

Office clutter is a deadly virus for which there *is* a cure. Read on!

A Cleaner's-Eye-View of Office Clutter

We cleaners probably see offices from a different perspective. Your own office or cubicle may be a little full now, but it's grown on you slowly over time. You know every last thing in there, down to a tiny scrap or note saved for secret reasons known only to you.

> "You'd love my boss's office—the stuffed toy hanging from the ceiling, a 'great white shark' with fake blood all around the mouth and a fish rear end hanging out the mouth; the stuffed parrot, the stuffed grouper, the stuffed dog that barks when knocked over, and the 2,000 files we can never find when an irate client is screaming on the phone. Not to mention phone messages from God-knows-when, and how to stop smoking and weight-loss tapes from 1995."

I, on the other hand, am a professional cleaner whose staff sees more than 40,000 different offices every week. We have to get around, under, over, and through every place in your office, not knowing and loving everything in it as you do, but simply cleaning it—and believe me, from that standpoint, it has a totally different look! Come visit some other people's offices and workspaces with me, and you'll see what I mean.

One time, I was touring one of the high-tech offices we clean. It was 9:00 P.M. and all thirty-one members of our cleaning crew were there. As the head honcho from headquarters, I spoke to them as a group, and then they headed off to their assigned tasks and their manager and supervisor began addressing some specific needs together. I was left to myself for an hour or so to wander through the endless rows of desks and offices. Because cleaning problems and frustrations seemed to be steadily increasing in all our office accounts over the last several years, I took out my yellow pad and began to look around. I started to record what was there, and it became clear just how far we'd come from the days of a simple desk, a chair, and a wastebasket!

This was a prestigious, nationally known company, but those workstations could easily have been confused with one of the local souvenir shops. There wasn't just one or two of something in any location, but whole selections of things such as coffee mugs, calendars, and clocks (including clocks with built-in barometers, thermometers, and hygrometers). The pens and pencils crowded into some kind of corral-like container rarely numbered less than two dozen.

I counted seventy-five teddy bears and their relatives—stuffed animals of every description—hung, shelved, clutched, or freestanding in those offices. (Not counting the teddy bear doorknob cover.)

There were knickknacks, trophies, and plaques every-where—everything from chenille-ball Garfields to idea light bulbs to marble honorable mentions. They covered the desks and any other horizontal surface, were stuck to the walls and the sides of file cabinets.

Posters! Posters! Posters! And pictures, pictures, pictures, nicely matted and framed or simply torn from old magazines or calendars and pinned up somewhere (enough pictures of water-falls, koala bears, and beach scenes to wallpaper a 200-story building). And signs! Many desks had enough signs around them to shame a city intersection: In, Out, TGIF, management and motivational mottos, organization charts that no one understands or reads, wedding or horse show announcements made into temporary signs, and framed documents with type so small your breath would fog the glass if you tried to read them.

Umbrellas, shoes, boots, jackets, and other extra clothes were stuffed everywhere. As for plants, some offices easily had enough to do on-location filming of *Jurassic Park*. Beside the flowers, dead and alive, were rows and stacks of stuff from seminars. (By all evidence, at least 10 percent of the occupants' time was spent in seminars and conventions.) The magazines piled around and over everything needed to be measured by how many feet deep, not how many. And as for catalogs, there were not merely a few dozen from the immediate suppliers of the company, but computer catalogs of all kinds and at least one copy of every popular consumer mail-order catalog from Lands' End to J. Jill.

Piles and stacks of papers covered the desks and tables, teetered on the tops of file cabinets, bulged from the inboxes, packed shelves and bookcases, and in some offices, even occupied half the floor.

An engineer would have paid a generous admission to see the ingenuity and variety of the tools and equipment these office folks had assembled—every type of sorter and In and Out tray ever invented. Any interest in creative paper clip holders would have been well satisfied in that night's tour; and once labeled a "paperweight," anything was legal on a desk, from bricks to bowling balls to miniature ingots. There were hand-held staplers, long-reach staplers, electric staplers, even copy machines with built-in staplers. As well as gadgets to load staples, to remove staples, to dispose of staples, and to store extra boxes of staples.

You could hardly find a ringing telephone under all the extras attached to them.

There wasn't just one computer per desk, but believe it or not, at many desks there were two, and of course, every imaginable attachment. Plus at least one whole closet just for programs, instructions, hardware, and software.

There were foot heaters, coolers, and massagers, and of course the "excer-clutter"—all kinds of paraphernalia to tone muscle and put cellulite to flight: hand squeezers, jump ropes, rowing machines, treadmills, stationary bikes. Radios were set in and around everything, and retired typewriters and unused portfolios were everywhere under the desks.

And then the munchies! Gadfrey, I could do an in-depth report on the eating habits of office personnel. Candy bars and Oreo cookies in the lower left-hand drawer, stale crackers, and enough stirrers and sugars, real and artificial, for at least

fifty gallons of whatever brew that particular desk jockey was addicted to. Pretzels, peanuts, potato chips, condiments. And then for the aftereffects: Alka-Seltzer, Tums, Tylenol, and other medications. If all the employees in the building pooled together, they could easily have stocked a drugstore.

At the ends of the halls, the corners of rooms, and under the staircases sat phased-out furniture—backless, armless, nicked, scratched, or just plain unneeded chairs, desks, tables, and lamps.

Behind, under, and around everything, like a den of hibernating rattlesnakes, were the electrical cords. They were bad enough in "P.C." (pre-computer) days, but now they were almost intolerable—a big bundle spread under every desk and over every floor to gather dead bugs, lint, and wrappers.

As I experienced firsthand the difficulty of getting through offices under these conditions, it was easy to understand why the cleaning was taking longer. More of everything, two PCs per person, and bumps and bruises just trying to get in and out.

When we reviewed this array of clutter in the average, everyday, all-American office afterward, the people assigned to service the area explained all the cleaning and maintenance problems it caused. Even the most careful, conscientious cleaner is bound to miss or break something in the masses of clutter in and around these desks.

Bosses and business owners frustrated with the proliferation of "stuff" have let consultants, architects, decorators, and salespeople lead them through everything from open office concepts to modular enclosed, from single to group workstations and back again, and to everyone's amazement, the men and women who inhabit the workspaces have, in minutes, found a way to re-establish and remultiply it all!

What's There?

✓ Jarful of stuck-together hard candies
✓ Mounted mallard duck
✓ Live-in-the-past trophy
✓ Never-used souvenir mug
✓ Uncomfortable executive chair
✓ Lamp that doesn't give enough light
✓ Plastic African violet

✓ Partial deck of cards
✓ Some scientific thing
✓ Pelican made out of split peas
✓ Photo of ex-girlfriend/ex-boyfriend
✓ Picture of the flat-screen TV employee is working to pay for
✓ State-of-the-art pencil sharpener (and no pencils)
✓ Wind-up clock with only one hand
✓ Jumbo bottle of ibuprofen with only three pills left in it
✓ Cigar box full of pens waiting for refills
✓ Bubble gum machine
✓ Miniature car model
✓ Plastic frog paper clamp
✓ "Stop on the way home" list from several months ago
✓ Unread memos
✓ Ignored phone messages
✓ Outdated agendas
✓ Ancient FedEx receipts
✓ Something brass
✓ Miniature putting green over in the corner
✓ Backpack or down vest to make her look outdoorsy
✓ Picture of the family decked out in antique outfits
✓ Pretty stamps torn from envelopes
✓ Busted manicure tools
✓ Incomplete mini sewing kits
✓ Copy of *In Search of Excellence* that has never been cracked
✓ Painted and stenciled wooden box, filled with clutter
✓ Eyeglasses from two prescriptions ago, with an earpiece missing
✓ Exacto knife, no blade
✓ Empty binders
✓ Paper clip holder with magnetic hands that pop out
✓ Soaps, mints, and peanuts from past business trips
✓ Memorabilia from his last job
✓ Things she's keeping for "ideas"
✓ Mail returned four years ago for a bad address
✓ Pizza discount coupons from three years ago
✓ X-ray of a starfish
✓ Empty Kleenex boxes

Your Three-Minute Desk Test

How to score: For each of the following statements, figure out which answer best describes you and write the corresponding number in the blank line next to the statement. Then add up the numbers and total them for your score!

5 = Always
4 = Nearly Always
3 = Sometimes
2 = Almost Never
1 = Never

_____ My desk is clear and unobstructed.

_____ I can find anything I need on it, in seconds.

_____ Others can find what they need there, in my absence.

_____ All the paperwork on my desk is current.

_____ I have no excess duplicates of anything.

_____ All fileables are filed.

_____ There's plenty of room in my workspace for new projects.

_____ I use everything I have on, in, and around my desk.

_____ All broken or inoperable things are gone.

_____ Everything on my bulletin board is current.

_____ I feel totally in control in my workspace.

_____ **Total**

55–40: You can feel good about yourself. It won't be long till your promotion!

39–30: You're an average, overjunked American.

29–20: You're not setting a good example. Stop misrepresenting the hard worker you know you are, and clean up your act!

20–11: Are you sure you still have a job? There's still a flicker of hope for you—read on!

If an office doctor were delivering a diagnosis on the average cluttered office, it would be "condition: serious." A dentist would call it "impacted," a lawyer "libelous," a safety engineer "hazardous to personal and job health," a minister "sinful," and you, well you already know—

IT'S TIME FOR A CHANGE!

Chapter 2
Why Change?

Here are some true-life experiences sent to me by readers:

"Because a vital letter from me was lost in a heap of junk by the Social Security Administration, my son's essential application for a disability allowance was delivered to a building that had been demolished two years before. Only the door still stood—with a letterbox on it."

"The 'loss' of a schedule for a trust caused a major client to go elsewhere. We found it five minutes after he walked out."

"Ever tried to find something the boss needs 'right now' when there's at least two months' worth of paper piled up on your desk?"

"We searched and searched and could not locate the corporate seal when we really needed it. Eventually, it was found in a drawer full of six years' worth of gift calendars."

"We found a five-year-old, uncashed insurance refund check for $800 amidst the five years' worth of old magazines on top of a desk."

"I bumped some boxes over and dumped 500 negatives on the floor. They absorbed water from a roof leak and were ruined."

"The cost estimate and correspondence on an important job got lost on the boss's desk, but the boss managed to make it to the meeting and BS his way through. Mr. Messy Desk convinced everyone that the job was ours. We started arranging everything to go through with it. Two months later, after lots of our time and money had been committed to this project, we found out the bid went to someone else."

"I was entrusted with some field notes for a project and dutifully put them away 'where they would be safe.' Then I couldn't find them and we had to re-create them. Then (to add insult to injury) we found them where they had waited safely. Plus my cohorts have long memories."

"About eight years ago, my husband withdrew from his union job to accept a supervisor's job with the same company. He received an honorable resignation from his union (very important for receiving retirement income after twenty years with the union). Yes, I misplaced it. For years, I was unable to throw anything away because of that darn paper, for fear it might be caught up in something else."

"I remember a delay in escrow at our bank because a lending officer couldn't find a title report in the total mess of all kinds of papers on her desk. We finally had to request an additional copy from the title company."

"I'm always accusing someone of having made off with something from my office. I usually end up finding it right where I left it and have to apologize."

"In my work as a sales associate, quotations and follow-through are everything. Many, many times I haven't been able to find quotes when my fellow salespeople were on the road. Many orders have been delayed or even lost because of poor organization and follow-through."

> "A client of mine was constantly stressed and passed over numerous times for a promotion as a result of missed deadlines and the inability to locate important materials when needed."

People would rather talk to you about their sex life than their paper problems. In comedies, cartoons, and even corporate meetings we all joke about the "dirty desk." It's an immediately recognized problem—generally someone else's. Yours and mine aren't perfect, in fact they're getting a little untidy, but it's those other desks and offices that really are a disgrace. Besides, my desk is *me*; that's just the way I am. I may heap and pile, save and stash, but I do my best work there. It may occasionally border on pandemonium, but it's not quite there. When and if my office and desk get as bad as everyone else's, I'll admit to the disease. Until then, I'll continue as usual and hope my new sign—*"A clean desk is a sign of a sick mind"*—will allow me to slide past any possibility of paper purging. The bad news, folks, is that our workspace speaks for and about us to everyone. We may accept its condition as "workable" or even comfortable, but we'd surely be shocked to see a copy of its report on us.

After all we go through to get a good job and then to better our image and position—draw up a resounding resume, drive an upscale car, join well-respected organizations, wear the latest styles, give to charity, and pay all our taxes—would our office really talk about us that way?

It will and it does; it keeps sending signals to everyone around us. It projects our ambitions, passions, and for sure our organizational abilities. I've seen some great arguments for handwriting analysis, how your penmanship reveals your real personality. You may believe that or, like me, think it's iffy, but you need not doubt that the pens in, on, around, and under your desk make a statement about you.

After more than forty-five years of professional cleaning, I'm convinced that a pretty accurate personality profile of any of us can be drawn just from our office and desk alone.

Just lean back in your seat right now and think about it: What kind of atmosphere does my workspace have, create, or leave with other people and even myself? Consciously or unconsciously, everyone feels something toward you while they're in your area—your authority, your ability, it may even be like looking up at Mount Rainier. If your office or cubicle happens to be more like looking down a landfill, it sure isn't working very hard on your behalf.

If I were the head of a Labor Qualification Committee for the country, my first official act would be a mandatory attachment to every resume or application for employment anywhere: a picture of your last desk and workspace on an average day. As a hiring prerequisite it would be right in there with nondiscrimination for sex, race, or national origin.

Lost!

I received a call early one morning from the building manager at Sun Valley Lodge, okaying a bid we'd given on the demolition of a worn-out wing of the lodge. He told me to drop by that morning to pick up a contract and get started. He was the nicest guy, but his office was a collection of not merely paper piles, but paper skyscrapers! Every project was a stack, and when he ran out of room on his desk he just kept adding tables, and then he went on to the floor. When I popped into his office he brightened and said, "Aha, Aslett," then started shuffling through the "fresh" twelve-inch pile of important-looking documents. He rustled and pawed and muttered, "Darn it, I just had it a minute ago." He hunted for fifteen minutes while I waited. Finally he threw up his hands and said, "Oh heck, I'll find it later. Just go ahead and get started." The bid had contained many important details, like who paid for the conveyor, how soon we could start, and the necessary noise abatement procedures. Without it, the whole day ended up a problem. We started at the wrong end of the building, and the security guards wouldn't allow our dump trucks to go through until they had permission from the manager (who was still thrashing around trying to find the four-page proposal). Our speed and accuracy—not to mention public relations—were shot by the end of the day, all as the result of one person's disorderly desk.

P.S. He did finally find the bid months later, tucked into a six-month-old ski magazine—he'd been using it as a bookmark.

> "A lot of people think clutter shows that they are busy. They are busy—looking through clutter for important stuff."

How many times has it happened to you, and how many disaster stories have you heard from dear friends with disorganized desks? How many times is something we really need—NOW—lost amidst the clutter? We label it "misplaced" or "mislaid," of course, but the result is the same. We know it was delivered to us or to our desk and it's there . . . somewhere. It causes not just embarrassment but also lost jobs.

How many late charges and penalties do you think are paid by people who didn't necessarily lack the cash to pay that bill, but simply lost track of it? I know real estate agents who lost sales because escrow information was buried and lost on their desks. And what's worse than leading someone to your desk and then having to flail around, frantically digging and rummaging through everything, to find the item you're after? Then you find it six days or six months later, right near where you thought you put it, only it slipped under or into another old pile. You're thrilled—it wasn't really lost—you just didn't have it when you needed it!

How many lessons, papers, lists, proposals, drawings, and plans have you had to do over from scratch because you couldn't find the original? I can't tell you how many of the college and high school students I've taught have come forth with that as the reason for their failure to produce a paper or report: "I lost my notes [or the assignment itself]." Big businesspeople and brilliant assistants do this too, mostly because of overloaded offices. You'll cut your losses when you cut the clutter!

The Biggest Loss in a Cluttered Office

Don't forget the biggest thing you lose from a cluttered, messy desk or office—**RESPECT.** Your desk is you. What assumption do people make about someone operating out of a cluttered, crowded, chaotic place? "I'd say he's lost control." "Looks as if her job is too much for her." Do you want your desk to make those kinds of announcements about you?

What would you think if you went to see a doctor and the whole office was strewn with castoff casts, removed appendixes, used syringes, discarded latex gloves, and dirty cotton swabs? Even if you were seeing the best surgeon in the world, you'd take your double hernia (and your business) elsewhere. Or if you stopped at a bank and could hardly find the teller's station for all the loose bills and change and statements and deposit slips strewn around. Or went to a carpenter's workshop and he'd never swept up the sawdust and scraps, was just wading through it all knee-deep. Or if you visited a car detailer and had to step across mounds of old parts, crumpled invoices, greasy rags, and puddles of oil to do so. You'd most likely deem them all incompetent. Well, if you have a cluttered office or a messy desk, that's exactly what everybody, including your fellow clutterers, thinks of you. Being thought of and treated as incompetent is more than most of us can take; it's about the greatest insult anyone can offer us. Surely now, this very week, this very day, you have time to prevent this.

"His office was so cluttered that instead of attempting to clean it we laid several boards down in the middle of it all and made it look like a construction site."

Papers lying around in piles and heaps don't just affect the quality of your own life. They cause much murmuring on the part of onlookers, who think you are heading an ongoing paper drive.

Clean speaks, and it says "I care, I appreciate, I have values, and I'm in control."

Sloppiness speaks too, and it shouts "I don't care, things are out of control, and I'll accept just about anything!"

Excess is always ugly, isn't it? Too many decorations on something, too much muscle on a bodybuilder, too much makeup on even a beautiful woman. Too much of even useful things (furnishings, supplies, tools, office help) is always cumbersome and negative.

Your workspace, desk, or office area isn't just your signature, it's a neon sign. It's a full-page ad of your attitude, ability, aims, and attention to things, in your work and in your life.

It's My Business, No One Else's!

How many times have we heard someone, even ourselves, say, "This is my desk and its condition is no one else's business or concern." Sounds downright "Bill of Rights" all right, but it might need some amendments:

1. First of all, most offices and cubicles aren't ours; they belong to someone else and we're just using them.

2. Let's not forget that offices are basically space and equipment allocated to perform a *job*.

3. Most offices are part of a company of some kind, so what they look like and how they run literally *is* someone else's business.

In most cases, when we're in an office, we're being paid to perform and produce. A contaminated workplace impedes that function. If we insist on remaining disheveled, we're ripping off our boss somewhere along the line.

It may not be said openly, but your value to your boss is being judged daily by a number of things, many of which are directly reflected in your workspace.

Speed—Bosses want speed, and junk and clutter slow you down.

Safety—Unsafe premises really cost the boss, and junk and clutter are a safety hazard.

Accuracy—Bosses hate mistakes, and junk and clutter affect accuracy.

Security—Anything unattended (such as piles of clutter) is very likely to get lost, tossed, misplaced, or snooped into. Clutter can never be "Classified," and litter surely doesn't have any lock on it!

Image—You want to project an attractive, positive, in control appearance. Junk and clutter give the WRONG image.

Cost of replacements and repairs—When there's too much stuff around, things are much more likely to get duplicated, broken, or stolen.

Cost of the space you occupy—Business owners pay a premium cost for office space, per square foot. Space buried in stuff is wasted, and bosses don't like waste!

Cleaning costs—It takes much more time, equipment, and material to clean a heaped and cluttered area. A junked-up office means more cleaning costs and problems (who would know better than me?).

Confusion—Has no place in an operation, large or small. Junk and clutter breed confusion.

Tension—A poorly kept workplace makes everyone tense, and who likes tension and stress?

Distraction—Too much stuff around is distracting, and no one wants his or her helpers distracted!

A messy desk, or even a neat one piled with clutter, is not only irritating to your superiors but is an engraved invitation to question your efficiency. And we all look like klutzes when we're pawing, digging, rummaging for something somewhere in our piles or files or briefcase.

The granddaddy of all management weaknesses is indecision. And the biggest sign that a crammed desk and office holds up is *"I can't make a decision.* I just keep it all, stack it up, shuffle it around, paw through it when I have to and keep hoping there'll be a fire before I get fired." Junk and clutter—too much of everything—booms out in a loud voice—*Indecision.*

Believe it or not, like it or not, what other people feel, think, and say about you does matter because they make judgments and decisions for and about you based on those feelings and observations. We've all passed up restaurants and service stations because of the way they looked or smelled; we've all sought out another motel or campground when the one we just walked into seemed littered or disorganized. Even if a place is clean but crowded and cluttered, we're likely to move on. Your office can have the same effect on others!

So why should you correct the situation?

SELF-PRESERVATION! Let's do it!

> "A cluttered office can be a form of 'protection' from being asked to do more. The person involved doesn't realize how much clutter impedes his work."

What a Messy Desk Really Costs the Company

Just for the fun of it, either alone or with a group in a staff meeting some time, go over the following list and fill in the blanks. It'll be fun and enlightening and surely cause the lightening of some desk dungeons, too.

_____ Percent of work time (and salary) lost to slowness, inefficiency, and confusion caused by clutter

_____ Percent of work time (and salary) lost to being distracted by your own junk

_____ Cost of customers lost because a messy desk put them off

_____ Cost of business opportunities lost because something lay in the pile too long, or was never noticed amidst the mess

_____ The "spectator cost"–the time lost by everyone else in the office walking around, looking at, talking about, and meeting about your heap

_____ Your own time and energy spent explaining, joking about, and making excuses for the embarrassing condition of things

_____ Overhead money (rent!) lost to space that's "lost in space" (so cluttered up it's useless)

_____ Furnishings, supplies, and equipment ruined (warped, bent, broken, smashed, rusted, or rotted) because they were crowded by, crammed with, or in contact with clutter

_____ Cost of extra gear (furniture, "organizers," etc.) to sort and store unnecessary stuff

_____ Extra safety insurance premiums made necessary by a cluttered workplace

_____ Extra cleaning costs for a cluttered workspace

If we just figure conservatively that junk and clutter reduce the efficiency of the average worker by a third, that's thousands or tens of thousands of dollars a year, and if we added in things like loss of customers over clutter, we could easily be up in the hundreds of thousands. The indirect costs of many a clutterer are surely greater than their whole salary for the year. Clutter is even more expensive than it is unsightly!

What Can a Messy Office Cost You?

We think we get away with just a few snickers or jaundiced looks, or maybe a little kind or unkind kidding. The real costs we never calculate are big ugly things like lost jobs, late or never completed assignments, alienated clients and customers, demoralized subordinates, injuries, and maybe even a failed marriage or two as well as the loss of confidence and self-esteem. Clean desks get promoted. Messy desks get nothing but grief.

Undone Paperwork Multiplies Itself

Need a little more incentive or motivation to get at that "undone" and "overdue" paperwork around your desk and office?

Just think of what happens when you have an unpaid bill. We've all had a bill we didn't pay right away. The minute we lay it back on the pile, it begins to multiply itself.

1. First it plugs itself into our consciousness and conscience and takes up space, adds some mental weight there.
2. Then we get a little dunning note, and then another (more paper for the pile).
3. Next we get calls and recorded messages about it.
4. Now we have to write a letter or make a call to explain the delay.
5. Now interest and penalties are added to it, requiring more complicated record-keeping and ledger entries.

6. Bill collectors begin to call.

7. By now, of course, it's on our credit report, where it will haunt us for the next seven years.

8. As time passes, yet more explanations are needed, and often by now a brisk argument or two. . . .

Soon this one simple bill is at least ten times its mental and physical size.

We may have an excuse for an unpaid bill—no money—but for most undone paperwork, not so. We have the time, if that's the issue; we just have to decide to withdraw it from our time bank. It's really ridiculous to wait for later to deal with most things. Later, it'll take three or four or fifty times the time to do it, and cost more, too.

The Proliferation of Paper

We're mowing the lawn. There in front of us is a piece of paper—a paper plate or crushed Dixie cup. The spirit says pick it up, but we're so comfortable and paper is no match for that powerful blade we control. Plus in little pieces, surely it will soon disintegrate (our contribution to recycling this week).

So we mow over it—Sfx! Thrunddnt!—and we get our wish. That once-easy-to deal-with single piece of paper is now 283 pieces, all over the place—a real mess to leave on top of a nice neat lawn. And now the two seconds it would have taken to deal with it is more like twenty minutes.

This is the same thing that happens as we mow through our office paper. What is left undone always gets in the whirly blade of busyness and multiplies.

When Bad Things Happen to Good Papers

Ever notice how papers left out and around collect not just dust but all kinds of other embarrassing evidence of their sojourn?

Then, if we're spared having to re-create the whole page or document, there is still the time and dignity lost trying to erase, wash, whiteout, or sticky-note over the evidence. So much simpler just to put things back as soon as we're finished with them!

Stains That Get on Papers

- Marker and ballpoint ink
- Toner, printer spatters, carbon paper smears
- Print rubbed off other papers
- Coffee, tea, cola (because we must have a cup of one of these by our side every minute to face mental labor)
- Salad dressing, grease from chips, sauce from pizza, etc.
- Blood from paper cuts
- Dirty fingerprints
- Footprints
- Paw prints
- Mildew
- Raindrops and tears
- Dust and cobwebs
- Squashed bugs

The At-Risk Office

By now you've heard plenty of reasons to free yourself of office excess and disorganization, and probably thought of a dozen more yourself. Here's one you might have missed: SAFETY. Do you know how many people slip and fall on fancy little rugs set on top of slick office floors? Fires and electrocutions, as well as bad shocks and burns, can easily result from plugging twenty gadgets into a two-plug circuit. How many back injuries are the result of heaving around heavy, awkward (and unnecessary) office stuff? How many hands are cut or punctured by weird stuff that shouldn't have been there, in an office, but it was? Boxes and containers piled high in storage have also unpleasantly surprised many. Partly drunk cups of coffee and soda left around here, there, and everywhere have caused tons of extra work for the office cleaners, and major damage to office machines. Piling things like stacks of paper and books on top of office machines like copiers, computers, and fax machines isn't just messy, it can cause them to overheat.

Janitors know well that it's hazardous duty to work around a cluttered office. You bump your shins getting in and around things, your vacuum cord catches on and tips over piles, you run into partly open (so full they can't be shut) drawers, and there's all kinds of hidden stuff to spill, fall over, or get cut on. A junked office about doubles cleaning time and risk. The sheer volume of all this worthless stuff means that sooner or later it has to be moved. That means bending and lifting, which means wrenches and sprains.

"Mess" means we don't know or remember what's actually there, and some of what we've lost track of is bad stuff—flammable or poisonous liquids or powders, oozing glue, leaking batteries, razor blades, needles, tacks, and other sharp hardware. I've seen dangerous solvents and other "don't know what to do with it" stuff left out somewhere in an office and everyone (wondering, just like you, what it is) comes by and picks it up, shakes it, opens and sniffs it, attempts to remove a spot with it, etc.

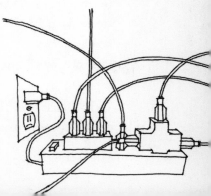

Even our miscellaneous display items can pose a threat. I remember one office we cleaned where a guy had a most attractive "candy dispenser" on display. It was almost impossible to walk by without wanting to snatch a piece. Problem was, it was actually a collection of quartz and other small, pretty polished rocks, and it broke a tooth or two in its time. Your exotic souvenirs and collections can easily injure an innocent guest or even a janitor.

Safety in the office isn't really an issue of whether your replica of a Henry VIII beheading ax might fall off the wall onto someone, however. It's a bunch of potential little problems all added up, and even one of them is too many.

The Rewards of Dejunking

"Why should I?" is the first question kids come up with when instructed (or ordered) to clean their rooms. Then they take a deep breath and go on with some other pretty good arguments.

"It's my room."

"I like it that way."

"I'm expressing myself."

"I can find everything I need to."

"I can still get through/across it."

"Why can't I do it later?"

"I have homework to do."

"Nobody has to go in there if they don't want to."

"I'm working on it."

"It's my problem."

"Look at Joey's room."

And at least fifty more creative reasons to justify the junk pile most kids' rooms are.

HERE'S A QUICK SAFETY CHECKLIST:

____ Anything stored on the floor?

____ Anything stacked on stairs?

____ Anything stored or piled up high or precariously?

____ Papers or boxes piled near space heaters, baseboard heaters, bare light bulbs, or other electrical equipment?

____ Clutter blocking access to fire escapes or extinguishers?

____ Any office furniture made top-heavy by all the stuff piled on it?

____ Any drawers (especially those crammed full ones!) missing stops?

____ File drawers so full the cabinet is out of balance the minute you pull one out?

____ Dangerously dilapidated furniture (such as rickety chairs) you've refused to part with?

____ Dangerous chemicals or objects such as sharp tools or weapons out or accessible?

____ Are you lugging things around that ought to simply be pitched? (As you've surely noticed by now, boxes of paper, old magazines, etc., are among the heaviest things going!)

____ Overloaded electrical outlets or extensions? Or cords in a position to catch chair casters or trip someone?

____ How secure are all those things hanging on the walls?

____ Do you ever put sharp or dangerous materials in the trash?

All we occupiers of offices were kids with rooms once, too, and we've brought all these excuses for our messes right along with us into adulthood. Rather than exist with or insist on these old pigpen platitudes, we ought to take a minute and think this through.

Feeling good and being treated well—what means more to us in life? Almost everything we do, buy, own, wear, and exert any real effort for is ultimately to feel good and be treated well. And guess what—being neat, clean, and organized will *guarantee* that we feel good and are treated well.

What more reason do we need to go after that cluttered office and conquer it? For the praises and raises, heed and speed we'll gain, the pride, the confidence, and the self-respect we'll reclaim!

> Decluttering is the simple, no-cost solution

But I Can't Operate Any Other Way!

Many people say in defense of dishevelment that if it were cleaned up, they couldn't find a thing.

> "I can't think in a neat, clean place.
> I need chaos to concentrate."

They might be conditioned to that now, but they'd be amazed how much better they'd like the opposite once they have a chance to experience it. It's like the people who claim to be a day or night person by birth. They have to go to bed at 1:00 A.M. and get up at 9:00. They've done it all their lives, and no change is possible. "It's just my metabolism," they say—and they really believe it. Then they get a new job or make a life change, and they have to go to bed at 9:00 P.M. for a 4:30 A.M.

commute . . . and not only do they adapt in a week or so, but they also love it and find a new life of real accomplishment out there in the early rising world.

I remember an engineer who was put in charge of a big new Bell system building that was under construction. The office he usually operated from was crammed and cluttered. With the new assignment he had to be on location for three years, so they moved him out of his big, fancy, ten-file-cabinet office to an on-site trailer. He had to do all his work out of a knapsack and one small desk right out in the construction area. He suddenly became quicker and more effective—even more likable. He didn't have to wade around in and maintain piles of stuff, and he was able to do his work in ⅕ the space and with ⅒ the equipment. He had no storage room or place for anything pretty and didn't have to worry about image—he loved it!

I made the same kind of discovery myself in grade school. Mine had all eight grades in one room, until eventually we expanded to four in one room and four in another. We each had our very own desk (not unlike our grownup situation). We had all the necessary tools and books and a constant flow of paper going in and out. Most of us were smart enough to keep the A papers and toss the Fs, but after that, into the desk went all of our art, notes, valentines, leftover lunch wrappers, ball gloves, etc. So even at this young age we had to deal with desk clutter and there were two basic choices: 1) Fix it, or 2) Fight it. Most of us chose the latter. When it was up to us, it all stayed and we just developed our skills of stuffing and stacking and prayed for a new and bigger desk next year. If we needed anything, we just had to paw around, grope, and hope. (Look at the average high school or college locker and you'll see the same condition today.)

I went through three grades of this, always having a dog-eared "Big Chief" tablet and handing in bent papers and losing my pencils in the mess. I had to pull and pry things out of my desk and often spilled ink in the process. I didn't deal with the flow of stuff. I just stowed it ever tighter in that little compartment that never gave any indications of expanding.

Then one day (probably because I'd just watched Mom neatly organize a dresser), I dejunked my desk. There was enough old, soiled, rumpled, and rotten stuff to fill a wastebasket. Then I lined up my books neatly in order of use within easy reach, and put my pencils, ruler, and protractor together alongside my tablet, etc. When I finished, it looked and *felt* good and there was room, room, room! Not only was I impressed with my nine-year-old discovery, but the teacher gave me a genuine smile and pat on the back and reported it to my parents as well, who took me to a *second* Roy Rogers show that month.

This clean desk business seemed to be a good idea, so at the end of every day, I began a routine. I processed my papers and straightened up my desk and left it looking neat. This eliminated hunting for things, ruined papers, and the constant need for excuses, and it gave me more time for baseball at recess, too. It gave me a real feeling of conquering and control to have my books neat, and never again did I get my wrist rapped with a ruler for spilling or breaking ink bottles. This same principle worked later on with toolboxes, pickup beds, and athletic lockers. "Neat and clean, no clutter" always enabled me to move fast and be efficient, and it gained me the respect of professors and peers.

Aren't we all looking for some fun, adventure, and excitement in life? Well, guess what: Being clean, clutter free, and well organized is what gives you the best chance of bringing those ideals to pass. Clean even has a direct carryover into your character; you can't avoid it.

What if all desks went transparent for a day and everyone could walk by and see everything we had inside? Wouldn't that be a hoot, or maybe a hurt? If you're having a little trouble getting motivated, just imagine your desk is transparent right now!

The #1 Excuse

What's the reason most often given for keeping an office in a cluttered condition? "No time to do it" (unclutter it). In 99 percent of office clutter cases, the owners of these man- or woman-fills will tell you they know it's bad, for sure it should be cleaned up, they know better and they want to have it right, but . . . they just don't have time. The bottom line is "I'm so busy, there isn't time to deal with it." They admit to the need and to a desire to be decluttered, then beg off of the job of betterment because there isn't time.

If we made a list of lame excuses for all life's problems, this one would be at the top. We don't have time to keep things in order, yet somehow we do have the time to deal with the consequences of disorder. We have plenty of coping and compensating time, but none for decluttering. I remember a chair in a nearby office that had sprung a spring in the seat. It would have taken the owner all of two minutes to get a pair of pliers and snip the spring, but she didn't have time. So, meanwhile, it snagged six pairs of pantyhose and three different suits of clothes, and she seemed to have plenty of time to explain to each passerby about the condition of the chair, and she even found a half-hour to make a creative warning sign and hang it on the chair.

In another office I watched a person whose ink pad had run dry take fifteen minutes a day to carefully test and reposition his rubber stamp on the pad in an attempt to get a proper impression. And when that failed, he'd painstakingly fill out the missing letters by hand with a pen. (There was plenty of ink just twenty feet away in the supply cabinet. A refill would have taken only a minute.) When I asked him why, he said he "just didn't have time."

Remember this: Little weeds in the flower bed or garden take just a few minutes to remove, but when they're left ("till you get time") and they get big, they take hours, require more tools and chemicals and energy to remove, and damage the flowers and vegetables in the process. And, worst of all, they have a chance to reseed. That first fifteen minutes is a far better use of your time.

How to Regain Hundreds of Hours a Year

How much time is lost to a messy office? If you added up the extra time it takes to locate things and work in and around a disheveled office, I bet you'd find at least a 20 percent efficiency loss. That means 400 hours of work time lost a year—every year! And that's just your own time—your coworkers, subordinates, and superiors lose time over your clutter, too.

> How many times have you started the day—spent that crisp, prime, most ambitious first hour—looking for something you need to begin an urgent project? And how many times did you interrupt yourself later, still looking for it?

It might take twenty or forty hours or even more to clean up the premises now, but once you do, you'll regain at least 400 precious hours. Then if you *keep* your office neat, you'll lose zero hours to clutter for the next ten years, which means at least 4,000 hours given back to the business, at least $40,000 to $50,000, or far more, depending on what you get paid. And that's just the obvious cash. If the time lost to mental and emotional irritations and depression over clutter were added in, we could be talking about a total bottom line boost of $200,000 or so over a decade. The world, or at least your whole life, could be changed!

No time to do it? How can you afford not to?

I'd Really Love to Do It ... But When?

Don't ever ask that question again, folks, because time isn't a question of having; it's just a question of using. You have as much time under your control as anyone else does or ever will. "I don't have time" is just a public announcement of indifference, so don't ever say it, because what it really means is "It doesn't matter enough to me." Then quit even thinking it to yourself, and you'll finally be making a solid step toward getting your office and desk shaped up.

You can be sure time isn't ever going to alter its course just for you, or elongate your hours and minutes so that you can deal with a dirty desk or workspace. And waiting for something or someone else, some event or circumstance to come along and push you over the motivation edge so that you can attack your accumulation, is pure daydreaming, fan-

tasy, a waste of that time you just said you don't have. Classifying your clutter caches into light, medium, or heavy and then attempting to prioritize them in with all the rest of your agenda is also just adding more to the time-wasting side of the ledger.

Do it now. There is nothing more important than clean and orderly—in office or in life. No doubt about it—*nothing*. Your speed and quality of output, your mental attitude, the opinion of others, all the principles of production and management, all await and depend on order. Period.

People are always asking if I could please inspire them, make them *want* to declutter and clean up their place. Neither I nor anyone else can make you want to do it, especially when it comes to hard-core accumulations like workspace clutter. I can only point out what you're missing while your head and heart are burdened with all those piles and stacks. If you don't want to be freer, happier, richer, better liked, and more efficient, I can't help you.

Chapter 3
Let's Do It!
Some Easy Places to Start

Forget any fantasy you have of a quick fix for your office clutter overload. We all do that, you know. Before really facing the problem and finding a workable solution, we come up with imaginative escapist strategies. We're simply going to "use up" all the old, hardened erasers and outdated letterhead and everything else that has to go. Or we're going to invest in some of those expensive space-age filing systems guaranteed to self-file and fix all. We imagine quitting or moving away from the mess, or lucking into an office mate or cube-mate who majored in office archaeology.

Let's not forget that most erotic of office organizing fantasies, our own custom roll-top desk, the extra-deep model. Why, then, regardless of the state or condition of our desk, if our boss buzzes by or when quitting time rolls around, we can just pull it shut—*thlatt, latt, latt, latt*—and it's all out of sight!

Well, to regain room, peace, respect, and efficiency, if you can no longer stuff it all in or under something, you might just consider kicking it out! The dream of a junkless, truly functional workspace is one fantasy you can realistically fulfill. It's downright exciting just to think about it!

The trouble is that most of us have never really faced our office and desk problem. We've been conscious of it, struggled with it, and every so often we've attempted to clean and clear our way through it for the sake of sheer survival. But a serious "What do I have to do to make this work" effort, we haven't made.

Dejunk! If your office has become a premature burial ground for you, it's time to move out the mess. Dejunk! Easier said than done, you say. You've been trying to do this for years? Well, "try" is the wimpiest word in the entire dictionary of accomplishment:

> *I'll try to be there . . .*
>
> *I'll try to pay you . . .*
>
> *I'll try to fly this 747 . . .*
>
> *I'll try to give you a face-lift . . .*
>
> *I'll try to get this office shaped up . . .*

What does "try" tell you? Absolutely nothing. Try is one of the biggest waste words in the world; I don't want to hear it from you again. So let's just do it, let's dejunk.

"When Should I Do My Office Decluttering?"

There you go again, asking when! If you have any choice at all, don't do it in public view or on company time. It will hurt you. People will think less of you, even lose confidence in you when they see you muddled in excavating and restoring and reorganizing. Worthwhile as it is, it momentarily only intensifies the impression of things being out of control, of your being someone who has to rummage around and dig out all the time. Public decluttering will only give your coworkers cause to comment or stand by like vultures to collect whatever you divest yourself of.

Dejunking during work time will irritate your boss, too. Seeing people thrashing around in messes they themselves have created annoys 100 percent of bosses. The reason is easy enough to understand—they feel as if they are paying you twice. They paid you to create the mess (which cost them dearly), and now they are paying you to undo it. (If you are a boss, you already know this.)

The boss doesn't want to hear about your clutter problem, because it isn't supposed to be there. That wasn't the deal when they took you on. They hired you to perform and produce work, not chaos and clutter. You aren't being paid to battle and talk about messes. You lose enough brownie points for having a messy desk in the first place, so cleaning it up on company time is salt in the wound.

Find some off hour, some Saturday or rainy holiday, or come in early or stay late to do your decluttering. Then when anyone comes around during office hours they'll see you in full function, and your efforts will only win praises. No one really wants to see all the gory details of how food is prepared, everything that had to happen first, before that steak or hot dog could end up on an attractive platter on the table. The same with offices—no one wants to witness the gutting of a messy desk!

I'd do it at some secret time and then keep quiet about it. Let the improved conditions speak for themselves.

All at Once or in Installments?

Your attack style is up to you. How, when, and how much have to suit your mental and physical limitations (and the amount of pressure you're getting from colleagues, employees, or higher-ups). Personally I've never liked installment plans when it comes to cleaning or decluttering. I like to tear into and tackle the whole place at once. (Of course, that's my whole lifestyle. When I played ball, I liked the tape ripped off my ankles in one big painful yank, while others would endure a thousand tiny pains for ten minutes.) The important thing is to get to it, target it, attack it, come to terms with it, or trash it. Go through a box or a truckload at a time, but go for it.

Where to Start

I don't want to meddle too much in your own personal office or desk; what you toss or keep is none of my or anyone else's business, not even your spouse or boss's. But as someone who has cleaned, owned, and moved offices for more than forty-five years, let me suggest some things to consider seriously.

Junk Bunkers

We all know what those freebie mugs we pick up at conventions and trade shows are—a place to pack pencils or pens—at least half of them long dead. These "holders" and hundreds like them are what I call junk bunkers—something that has space to store more things than you need.

Junk bunkers are disguised and dignified by names like desk organizer, workstation organizer, desktop sorter, stationery organizer, closet organizer, drawer organizer, tool organizer, "banker's box," "space saver," "pigeon holer," "file extender," and magazine rack . . . all kinds of tempting little bins and boxes and dividers that offer us more stashing places than we have stuff. Rather than let that space go to waste, we cram something in there, ordaining it a "keepable" just because there is a place to keep it. Stacking trays are the  thoroughbreds of workspace junk bunkers, and cheap filing cabinets aren't far behind. Desk drawer organizers, too, have ten intriguing slots you'll find *something* to fit in.

Bunkers are a sure way to multiply your desk and workspace clutter. An elemental principle of decluttering is to let the junk bunkers be the first to go!

Anything Miniature (Capsule Clutter)

Somewhere along the line, the idea of miniaturizing seemed like salvation to frustrated office folk. Just make it smaller, more compact, and then it'll take up less room and we can keep it around. Or, if we can't afford the real, full-size one, then we can at least get a miniature one. We all fall for this—every time I see something miniature, whether it's binoculars, wrenches, knives, measuring tapes, or flashlights, I covet it and start imagining just where I'd put it in my home or garage or office.

A friend of mine had a little red plastic case about the size of a large spice can, for example. When he opened it, wow, there was a whole miniature office: a little pair of scissors, a six-inch plastic ruler, a tiny stapler, a little container of four thumbtacks and twelve paper clips, a tiny roll of scotch tape on a minidispenser. There was even a one-hole punch and a tube of glue.

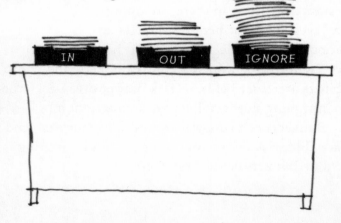

When I first saw it I drooled over it. What a fine little kit to have for traveling, for my spare desk, even for the car. I looked all over for one, and right in the midst of my longing and searching, one came in the mail from a friend for my birthday. I was elated . . . and now the proud possessor of one of the most worthless pieces of junk I've ever owned.

Almost nothing miniature ever really works; it's usually just a poor (not as well made and well engineered) substitute. The scissors in that tiny office outfit were dull and cut crookedly, the stapler could penetrate only about a sheet and a half, the only thing the glue stuck together was my fingers, and in five months of carrying that kit, using my best creative juices, I never found a single use for a six-inch ruler. The thumbtacks rolled out onto the floor of my hotel room one day when I was in a hurry, and the paper clips were soon all bent into sculptures during anxious phone calls. The tape dispenser broke on about the sixth pull. And every time I took something out of the miniature office kit to use it, it took at least half a minute afterward to fit it back into its little indentation in the case.

So I junked it, and good riddance to it all. . . . Of course, I kept that little case for a while "to keep loose change in"— until I came to my senses, and then I tossed it too. (Actually, I finally did find a use for the little ruler—I had to scrape some dog doo off my shoe in a hurry one day!)

By the way, how is your miniature calculator? Neat, isn't it, a calculator that fits on the back of a credit card or a business card or on your wristwatch or even mounted on a pen. Problem is, our big fat fingers can easily hit the wrong buttons of even the full-size ones, and we all know what they can do here!

Little things generally just don't work for big jobs. Perhaps you've learned that, too, but I thought I'd share this with you in case you're still pining for some cute little thing to save desk space.

Buy and use good office tools; go for the mighty instead of the miniature. Get the big full-size instrument you need to get the job done.

Empty Containers of Anything

Glue, ink, paint, polish, spot remover, Pepto-Bismol, prescription pill bottles, hand cream, ChapStick. In case you're wondering, yes, dried up counts as empty! (My editor found forty-seven dried-up bottles of correction fluid in her desk, though she wouldn't admit to this or dispose of them till after she'd switched to a word processor and thus was sure she'd never have to try to reconstitute them.)

The Containers Themselves

A hard-to-part-with category for any good clutterer is the container itself—the boxes that anything (stationery, envelopes, paper, CD-ROMs, film, throat lozenges, the space heater, the minirefrigerator, that floor-to-ceiling room divider) came in. Aside from the containers we keep just because they're cute—such as pen boxes and the little clear plastic boxes parts come in—in theory much of this is reusable. But, in fact, most of us never get around to reusing them, so we end up with aged mounds and piles of dusty, stained cardboard boxes, JiffyBags oozing gray globs, scattered plastic peanuts, half-popped bubble wrap, bent cardboard pieces, and mashed mailing tubes. The storage room, too, has old wooden crates and giant rug tubes and the bulky cartons every component of the computer came in, complete with one-of-a-kind, custom-fitted Styrofoam packing—a fire hazard and rat and roach haven!

At home, most of us have more space and excuses for keeping stuff like this—in the office, if you can't use it now and the shipping department doesn't want it, out with it!

We all keep mailing tubes, intending to use them for remailing. Meanwhile they become trumpets, megaphones, telescopes, or flyswatters—usually getting damaged in the process, so they should now be easy to dispose of.

Unnecessary Duplication: Tools

Yes, there can be too many of even a good and useful thing! You might need two or even three pairs of scissors, but surely not six! Same goes for staplers, staple removers, erasers, paper clip holders, rulers, and notepads.

Likewise, most of us need only one or two colors of highlighters, not seventy-two. And how many letter openers, pearl-handled or otherwise, do we need in this era of faxes, e-mail, and voice mail?

Getting rid of excess duplicates is one of the easiest dejunking details. Just go through and pull out all the things that do the same job. Lay them out beside each other and let the spirit move you as to which you really need and like. Then give the rest away or return them to the supply cabinet. Remember, less crowding means less time spent shuffling and hunting, fewer wrinkled reports, and more room for something fresh and new and better.

Unnecessary Duplicates: Photocopies!

"We do a lot of rephotocopying because we can't find something or are afraid we will lose it in the clutter, so we end up with numerous copies—more clutter!"

"One of the greatest clutter creators of the century—everyone needing 'their own copy.'"

Copies were once so difficult to make—and costly and ugly, too. Now a river of extra copies can flow out almost free (even in color), and they're often better looking than the original. So in addition to all the already too many copies we're supposed to make, we make several more "just in case." This is a good habit to break.

And an easy way to thin files and piles: *out* with everything except one good, clear copy. (Okay, in special cases maybe two, if you insist.)

> If we stacked up our extra copies of memos and
> FedEx envelopes I wonder how long it would take to
> reach the moon—probably at least till Friday, eh?

That "To Read Someday" Pile

"Someday" doesn't stretch on as infinitely as it once did in our lives. In fact "sometime" (thanks to our advancing age and the ever-increasing deluge of new stuff) is actually "no time," or *never*. So pull out those piles of old magazines and newsletters and memos, and all those clippings or articles someone sent or routed to you. If you can't get to them before the next full moon, compost them.

Aged-Out Stuff

Those things on which time has taken its toll—stuff that's dried up, rolled up, curled up, beat up, flattened out, crumpled, faded, frayed, rusted, cracked, unstuck, stained, yellowed, hardened, outdated, expired. Samples that were never sampled, never-opened packages of typewriter erasure tape, old, cracked chewing gum, and melted cough drops.

Look around your work area right now. How many things do you see that are clearly and officially dead, without the slightest trace of pulse or purpose? We all have some secret little hope that the unworkables will be resurrected. You haven't seen any of the occupants of the pyramids pull this off yet, nor will you see any use for old, outdated, dead office stuff. Hold a giant funeral today and bury the dead.

Parts to Something Long Gone

Many tools we use at home—from vacuums to cake decorators to sewing machines—come with attachments, something to hook onto and use with them. When the main unit finally dies, what do we do with the attachments? Keep them, of course. Why? "Because they've hardly been used; they're brand new." The same thing happens in the office, so we end up with drawers and supply cabinets full of electrical connectors, covers, and all kinds of attachments and accessories for long-gone equipment.

There are plenty of orphaned refills around, too, such as ink cartridges, staples, typewriter ribbons, adding machine tape, photo film, paper for binders and notebooks we no longer use. They may be good as new, but they won't fit anything we have now or will ever have again.

Old Calendars

You know, the ones with the nice pictures. It doesn't make them any more worth keeping if they have never-used diaries or appointment books for 1998 attached to them, or a complete guide to how many pounds of different seed are needed per acre (since you live in the suburbs). See page 154 if you need further convincing.

Old or Unused Appointment Books

Monogrammed, leather-bound or not, interspersed with pretty pictures or reproductions of antique prints or not, if you've never used it and never will use it, why are you keeping it? (Three or four entries in a year don't count.)

Anything Misprinted, or with Obsolete Addresses on It

Stationery, letterhead, envelopes, business cards, rubber stamps, return address labels, order forms, deposit slips. I know you have these slated to serve as your scratch paper till 2010, but the longer you keep stuff like this around, the greater the risk that

someone will accidentally use it. (This category includes those three sheets of stationery and two postcards you have from every hotel or motel in your business travels.)

That rubber stamp with a spelling error—I could save it to use in a pinch, or cover it up with tape, or cut the error off with a razor blade.

Seminar Sludge

Binders, booklets, articles, charts, tapes, questionnaires, agendas, scribbled exercises you did on the spot, free samples, etc.—all from sessions you slept most of the way through.

Convention Freebies

The minute we hit the floor of that huge hall we start filling those tote bags with abandon, with anything anyone is giving away, anything that's free. Then months and even years later we wonder where all these crushed posters, battered brochures, crumpled photocopies, meaningless business cards, stale fortune cookies, and boring or embarrassing lapel buttons came from. Grab one of the six tote bags in this stash and pack it all back out!

Nonfunctional/Defective Writing Instruments

Dried-up felt tip pens (no hope of a transfusion), leaky ballpoints shaped like curlicues or flamingos, pens that change their ink color to match your mood, pencil stubs, eraserless pencils you always pass over, mechanical pencils you never use and for which refills would be unavailable even if you did, grease pencils you've never actually been sure what to use for, that imitation quill pen outfit you picked up somewhere, the platinum-plated gift set too nice to ever use, etc. (While you're at it, eliminate anything over one spare cap for any type of pen.)

Obsolete or Unused Equipment

From old hard drives and calculators to slide rules to those fine old fountain pens and the manual typewriter that was your only office machinery for so long. Move it to your or someone else's antique collection if you must, but get it out of your badly needed working space. (And stop pretending that you're ever going to go back to using it.)

This category includes brand-new modern stuff too. If you can't or won't actually put it in use, move it on to someone who will.

Keys You Can't Identify, or to Places or Things You No Longer Own

We all have at least two dozen of these, between home and work. (No, they won't make you a fortune as scrap metal, so you can stop saving.) Test out all those keys; label them as soon as you rediscover what they open, and eliminate the rest. Scrap those old security access passes and hotel room keys while you're at it, too.

Pieces of Broken Office Furniture

Drawer knobs and drawers, lamp parts, armrests, headrests, desk or table legs, casters, bases, backboards. (The repair department of a modern office furniture store wouldn't even know what some of these things were if you brought them in.) If you can't fix it or even remember what it belongs to, get rid of it.

Office Husks and Hulls

Almost every office has some boxes or cases something valuable came in or was meant to be displayed, stored, or carried in. For a while you did take the time to keep taking it out and putting (strapping, clipping, fitting) it back in. But eventually you realized that if you were going to use it, you really needed it out and ready to go. So you finally quit casing or repacking it, but of course you kept the case or box. Because it was "the original box," you might someday need to repack or reship the item in it, or it might somehow otherwise be useful. And it's so sturdy, too. (But bulky and awkward to keep around.)

This category includes holders and dispensers of any kind that didn't work or that have since been superseded by a newer and better model. If it's something you really must or should keep, at least banish it to a storage area where it won't be in the way.

Outdated References

Almost every office I clean has the last three years' worth of catalogs and phone books, right alongside the brand-new up-to-date ones. We all have directories, books, maps, manuals, data sheets, price lists, and other references that are outdated and inaccurate, or from which we use only one or two pieces of information anyway. They can go anytime, and now is an excellent one!

Those "I'm Working on This" Projects and Piles

Not as impressive an excuse when the piles in question are six, twelve, or eighteen months old, or older. There finally arrives a time to do it or do without it. Past projects get harder to pursue as each day passes—those "in limbo" projects have usually gone limp and are blocking the fresh and new. It's time to pull them out, analyze, and activate or dump them to make room in your desk and destiny for what's coming.

Neat Things That You Never Use
(and May Not Even Know How To)

From paperweights and paper spikes to fancy bookmarks, from map-marking flags to cuff guards and calligraphy sets. How many desks, for example, still have a plastic triangle or a protractor and compass in the middle drawer somewhere?

Worn Out in the Drawer!

Every time I do, or witness, an office-cleaning project, I'm always amazed at how many things we come across that have never been used, yet are worn out . . . from being kicked around and shuffled around for years. Like tabs or labels (all types and colors) for file folders or drawers, stamp lickers, covers (for everything from calculators to computers), drawer dividers that didn't fit the drawer, gift pen and pencil sets, staple strips now in 100 pieces, off-size rubber bands, and greeting cards now too dog-eared and dirty to use.

• • • • • • • •

Wrong Place Clutter

It may be good stuff, but if it's in the wrong place it's still clutter! I see windshield scrapers, spark plugs, nuts and bolts, telescopes, fishing tackle, children's toys, chopsticks, paint paddles, and all kinds of other things taking up good working and storage space around offices. So right now, today, box up all that good but wrong place junk, take it away, and put it all where it really belongs and can be used. It's a great way to gain room for new projects.

Rough Drafts

They're the original blood, sweat, and tears often still resting there on the same shelf with the shining end product. It seems downright disrespectful to dump them—so we keep them. Plus, if you become famous they always want your papers, so who knows. . . .

Keeping the roughs (long after the polished and finished has gone on to its reward) isn't just a waste of precious space. Many projects go though multiple drafts, and this will eventually create confusion as to which one is the final one. When you're sure you have everything you really *do* need saved and right, take down the "scaffolding" and get rid of it.

Dead Sea Scrolls Junk

Old pages of indecipherable notes, sketches, and etchings we produced in intense, seemingly important moments. But for the life of us there's no way we can now read or translate them. We kept them, hoping a Rosetta stone might surface to illuminate them. (It didn't.) So, think on it a while, and if no enlightenment comes, dump them.

Snitched, Borrowed, and Never-Got-Around-to-Returning-It Stuff

Here's a dejunking detail that clears our conscience as well as the drawers: trays, silverware, and salt shakers from the cafeteria, the umpteen extra packets of ketchup, mustard, and taco sauce we snatched up and stashed away (now fermenting in our desk drawer), bundles of paper towels from the restroom, things people sent us as samples of their work (that we need to return because it was their only copy), books that belong to friends, colleagues, or the library, etc.

Anything Soiled or Spoiled

The pile of magazines the roof leaked on, the ceramic chicken with a broken beak, the candle shaped like Mount Rushmore that the office mouse chewed. Even hardened clutterbugs, thank heavens, hate to keep wrinkled, crumpled, frayed, faded, stained, dirty, or defaced things.

Chapter 4

Don't Stop Now: Keep On Decluttering!

You've got a running start now; you're beginning to feel the joy of being a born-again ex-junker. Don't stop now!

Tools and Accessories You Don't Really Need or Use

I see all kinds of things in offices, from paperweights to lamps to scales, that people don't use or even like, yet they keep them there because it's expected or it was there when they arrived or because it's "office-y."

Some of the tools and gadgets we have at our desks are there just because everyone else has one, or it was a mistake to buy them but now we have to justify our bad judgment. For at least a dozen years I bought and kept rubber cement in my desk drawer. I never used it, but whenever the bottle would dry up (usually because a borrower left the lid loose), I bought a new one. What for, I never stopped to think.

I bet I've owned at least twenty different devices designed to suspend a telephone from the neck, shoulder, etc. I broke more phones that way (when they fell off the holder and hit the floor) and cut off some important calls. Now I've found and use the most efficient tool ever invented for the purpose—my hand!

Likewise, we've all owned at least several business card holders. (I'm on number sixteen, myself.) None have ever worked; they're always too big, unhandy, or it takes an act of Congress to get the cards out or put them back in. If you run into one that really works for you, I'd like to see it! Right now I'm using the model that's served best for me on the road or at the desk—a rubber band.

"Desk sets" are a real pain in the blotter, too. Once the pen walks off (everyone always knows it's there, to snatch up in an emergency), the set is useless. Pen sets take up a lot of room on the desktop, too, and to outdo the competition these days they usually come with a built-in thermometer and barometer, or pulse and blood pressure checker. Gads! Just one more thing to clean around. But if you have an office, you'll end up with one or several of these, as going away, coming aboard, or length of service presents—like so many not-really-useful things, they're often gifts. I kept one on my desk for fifteen years just because it was "desk-y" and everyone else had one. I finally got tired of swiping pens from Hilton and Marriott to replenish its vacant slot, and just got rid of the whole thing.

Electric pencil sharpeners are another example. These should have been called "pencil shredders" because they can consume an entire pencil in about two sharpenings (or even just one, if you don't keep your wits about you). Even if we do actually still have a need to sharpen pencils, these plug-in wonders don't work as well as the old hand-crank model for most of us, and in any case one electric sharpener could probably service a whole floor of offices. Yet there are thousands upon thousands of electric pencil sharpeners across the land.

List Your Way to Clean

Make a list first thing some morning of "what my workspace is for"—the actual work functions—everything you do there that really counts. Then make a second list of all the things (furnishings, knickknacks, and equipment) you have in the work area. When you're done, go back through that second list and cross out anything that doesn't make any real contribution to the cause. You'll be surprised how little is left.

• • • • • • • •

Nonfunctioning Tools and Equipment

We all seem to have a weakness for that which worked well once but doesn't anymore. Almost every one of you, when asked what ridiculous thing you have around that does you no good, reported something broken—but that you "plan to fix someday."

One of the real Hall of Fame Classics of office clutter we hang on to, for instance, is the swivel chair. They often worked fine for quite a while. Then a caster falls off when we lift the chair one day, but just like fixing a faithful horse's hoof, we're willing to jump down on all fours and replace the caster and just be a little more careful from then on. When the chair begins to tilt or keel over backward, we price a new one and decide we can still live with the minor ailments ours has. Finally, it starts coming apart whenever we move it. This, too, we can accept—we just don't move it so much. Then its hip joint goes, and the chair snaps in two. But there it lies, the arms still good and solid, and the fabric on the back like new. It's dead, all right, but we can't bear to bury it, so we put it in storage or take it home!

People often ask me for the "real secrets" of time management and top production. *Having nothing around that doesn't work* is right at the top of the list. What good is something that doesn't work? Zero—in fact, it becomes a liability the minute it quits working. My New Year's resolution a few years ago was to own nothing that didn't work. I went on a slimming diet to reduce my overweight of broken, nonfunctional office and shop assets and lost 6,000 pounds in two months. (Counting the old vehicle that went, too.)

So right now, fix it or get rid of it. Do one or the other—whichever makes the most sense emotionally and economically. Fix it or get it out of your office—now, today! Even if two of the holes on the three-hole punch still punch perfectly, unless you're able to find someone willing to rebore that recalcitrant cylinder, it's out!

Broken Office Equipment That Is Often Kept

- Chairs, regular and folding
- Desks
- Bookcases
- Clocks
- Projectors
- Easels
- Typewriters
- Calculators
- Recorders
- Electric pencil sharpeners
- Electric staplers
- Collapsing coat racks
- Contrary copiers
- File cabinets with crippled drawers
- Jimmied locks
- Printers, scanners, portable hard drives

Fix it or nix it!

Excess Office Furniture

This is another big one. Sure, you might get an office, a bigger cube, or even a bigger office and need it some day, or someone else may show up and need it, but for now, instead of walking around it, bumping into it, and being crowded every day of your life by it, get it out of there and into storage. Be on the lookout for:

- Extra chairs (every office has some)
- Extra desks
- Unused tables
- Old typing stands
- End tables
- Lamps
- Couches
- Magazine racks

- Shelves or partitions that have never been put up
- That old sideboard that needs refinishing
- Drafting equipment

Do you know what the biggest hang-up is here? Status, again. Too many people think that once they have something, it's in their power—they're reluctant to let something of "theirs" go somewhere else or into the public domain. It's not what you have but what you get done that makes your reputation in the end. So just go right through and move out the good but unused today. It'll be like a long drink of good, fresh, cold Idaho spring water.

Clothes Clutter at the Office

Heading to the office in the morning is like kids going out to play on a nice spring day (albeit usually with less enthusiasm). Off comes the apparel as the temperature goes up! Kids toss theirs on the ground, or anywhere. We tuck ours under our

desk or into a drawer, or drape it over the back of a chair or an office partition. Or hang it up to age on a hook or rack somewhere. We're going to wear it home, of course, or maybe just keep it on hand here in case we need it, kind of like a second clothes closet.

Shoes (flats, heels, boots, sneakers, etc.) are the worst. But rain and golf gear and gloves and socks are right in there, too, along with the hats with the bent brims, extra sweaters, jackets, and coats. And the spare pantyhose "with only one run," that suit jacket or vest we never liked anyway, and the company T-shirt we wouldn't be caught dead in.

The bottom line is, seldom do we dress ourselves from the office. We fail or forget to wear home all that we wore in, and soon have multiples on hand. (The desk drawers usually have some shed jewelry in them, too.)

Gather up all this right now, and return it to its rightful place—home base.

Souvenirs

I've seen offices without windows, without files, without chairs, and even without desks. I've even seen some pretty productive offices without heat or electricity. But in my whole life I've never, ever seen an office without some kind of mementos or souvenirs Some bizarre things we've picked up along the way or been given will be found in any office. Even a roadside apple peddler in his rustic office has a one-of-a-kind contorted branch mounted on the wall for all to see. (When I worked at Sun Valley Resort, the manager had the biggest, nastiest pair of frayed ski lift cables on display right there in his office.)

You name it, and you'll find it in an office somewhere: skulls, musket balls, telephone pole insulators, bronzed baby shoes, rubber alligators, armadillo shells, street signs, sheep shears, high school scoreboards, old water heaters and shortwave radios, cast-iron bathtubs, peacock feathers, cross sections of trees, hockey helmets, golf trophies, and toilet clocks (guess whose!), artifacts without end or in some cases, name.

When it comes to souvenirs, I'm all for 'em. They give a workspace character and class. I love offices with some indication that the occupant has a pulse. Decoration like this does make a declaration about you.

But **IF** you keep it, be sure to somehow or other display it up out of the way of traffic. You sure don't want an autographed baseball rolling around on a desk or table you're trying to use. And a papier-mâché shark right over your shoulder will only distract you or slow you down. Hang it high, enclose it, laminate it, even buy a glassed table or museum case or shadowbox if you have to, but get it out of the work stream. Besides, if you leave your mementos out, they're sure to get lost, broken, or stolen.

Holiday Hangovers

Rare indeed is the office that doesn't have a stash of holiday gear—usually stored in a topless box somewhere, either totally forgotten or always in the way. Some of this is indeed worthwhile stuff, but most of it gets more wear and damage in storage than it ever does in use. We take it down in a hurry and cram it in a corner somewhere instead of putting it away. It ends up so beat and bedraggled it subtracts, rather than adds, to the spirit of the holidays.

First, weed through and get rid of any taped, glued, or tired stuff—all those old cards, ripped cardboard turkeys, crushed crepe paper pumpkins, frayed flags, faded flock bunnies, broken reindeer, melted candles, half-gone garlands, hopelessly snarled Christmas lights, unhangable ornaments, and untrustworthy tree stands. Then take all the rest, the decent, keepable stuff, and buy yourself one of those nice big plastic storage boxes. Fill it up with the truly active stuff and then label it clearly before you put it away.

Too Many Homey Touches

If we use our workspace long enough, regardless of what or where it is, we begin to feel at home there. There's a psychological comfort factor in that, and it can be a really good thing, but slowly converting our workplace into a physical duplicate of our home space can get to be a tricky business. We start with a work climate and then gradually change the atmosphere until our desk's real purpose is downplayed so much, you'd hardly know it's for working. This is one of those fine-line judgments, and the evolution is often so slow our boss and colleagues might notice it, but not us.

Take photographs, for example. Once, we had a single picture of the partner/spouse and/or kids on the desk. Now we have whole family trees, individually framed action shots of each kid or grandkid (plus one of the babysitter), fishing, and vacation pictures—and of course, the cat and the dog and the cockatoo. I've seen desks with thirty photos on or around them! We all want to feel at home in the office, and it can even be a good thing to have a reflection of our off-hours enthusiasms and interests here. But we don't want to make it look too much like a living room for relaxing, for at least three reasons:

1. All the extra junk and clutter this inevitably brings
2. The distraction potential, for you and other workers
3. The irritation it causes others to see the wrong kind of image projected

When you go to work and bedeck your office with radios, needlework or other personal projects in progress, or the raffle tickets you're trying to sell on behalf of your son, your boss is going to resent it.

A workstation isn't a storage bin, lunchroom, lounge, or rec room. A personal touch or two is okay, but I've cleaned many desks that have two dozen of them. This not only means extra cleaning, but much lingering and nonwork conversation spurred by the photos or keepsakes.

Sentimental Clutter, Office Edition

The office environment often outdoes the home as an opportunity for exposure to new friendships, relationships, discoveries, and accomplishments. Homes get warm thanks and maybe a card in the aftermath, but offices get hardware in the form of trophies, plaques, certificates, photos, bouquets (in keepable cheapie vases and baskets), candies (in keepable boxes), mugs, bottles, key chains, watches, pen sets, caps, jackets, buttons, badges, ribbons, pins, and gold-plated golf balls. Much of this clutter falls under that all-too-sacred category of keepables, "a gift from someone" (see page 117). Then we bring some of the sentimental overflow from home, too—stuff we couldn't bring ourselves to display there, such as those cute things the kids made out of popsicle sticks and elbow macaroni at school or camp.

When it comes to anything sentimental, remember you don't need a *thing* to hold on to a *feeling*.

Don't take it back home; recycle it. Most stuff like this can quietly be given to visiting kids, who will love and savor it and soon break it or wear it out.

If it really is good stuff, too dandy to dump, do what I finally did: Make a glass case or shelving for it somewhere so that everyone can get a good look at it. It'll also be out of the way and well protected from curious hands, dust, and damage.

Computer Clutter

There has been a lot of talk about the "paperless society," all the bulk and space we were going to save in the office. I haven't noticed a single condensation of clutter since computers arrived, only enlargement.

The day I brought the first computer into my office was exactly like bringing a rabbit home. Computers are frisky and fertile, and they fill everything . . . fast. Within days, cords to printers, monitors, and all kinds of other auxiliaries went everywhere. Today with the advent of USB as a power outlet, any piece of hardware can be plugged in, and peripherals can spread like wildfire—lights, external sound cards, speakers, hard-drive MP3 players, hot-sync cables, new readers for the flash memory cards that go in digital cameras, and PDAs—turning your computer into a Medusa of cables.

Computers led to the need for all kinds of special new furniture and supplies and accessories and storage facilities, and this soon meant platoons of a new breed of employee from the IT department who left in their wake servers, software, and interfaces that never ended. This in turn meant more insurance, more manuals, more huddles over mysteries and malfunctions, and more computer-bashing break conversation that never ends.

> "I have older versions and updates and patches for everything from Windows 95 to 98 to 2000 to XP. It's hard to part with the official looking hologram on the box or the manual that I really don't need anymore."

Computers mean more seminars to go to, too, and an ever greater concern for backup capacity. Back on day one, my assistant's desk had a sharp-looking case that held eight diskettes. Then floppies became SyQuests, then Zips, then CDs, then DVDRWs—each needing to be contained, sorted, cataloged, and backed up. One recent system may sound almost amusing to some, like overkill to others: RAID (redundant array of independent disks) has data backed up on five different disks, so that in the event of a crash or meltdown, at least one of the five will be retrievable! And throwing away outdated backup media is more traumatic than throwing away aged-out life preservers.

The computers themselves can all too easily become clutter, too—the lifespan of the average one is about three-and-a-half years. A $2,000 unit and all its accessories, still working like new, can be worth $500 overnight after the latest battle in the processor speed wars. It used to be that the difference between your old model and the new upgrade could be a 300 percent improvement. Not now. We've leveled off, and a new model may only be 10 to 20 percent better.

The latest, most powerful machine is usually a lot more than what most people need. The speed of processing video is not on the list of most of us, who just want to look up stuff on the Internet, type up reports and memos, and send and receive e-mail.

There are all kinds of hand-held, carry-with-you computers and cell phones today that store data—names and addresses, phone numbers, photos, notes and documents. They often hook right into your regular computer to exchange information. The downside can be that the screens are very small and hard to read, and the keyboards are small and hard to use. These minis, too, have their own clutter: built-in pens, extra cradles, cell phone chargers, batteries, cases, holders, clips, boxes, and instruction manuals—who wants to use a manual with a phone!

Some Common Computer Clutter

- Backup disks and backup, backup disks
- Disks that you can't open
- Disks with titles you can't remember
- Disks with outdated programs
- Outdated computer instruction manuals in mint condition
- The tractor-feed paper your printer no longer uses
- Burned CDs without labels
- Unlabeled disks by the drawerful
- Orphaned wires and cables
- Extra mice that don't work
- Out of date peripherals and hardware
- Shaky monitors
- Pristine packaging from original programs
- Holders and cases for floppies and CDs and all manner of portable media

Cutting Computer Clutter

Fortunately, the big boys (Intel, IBM, Microsoft) are beginning to tackle the problem of computer clutter, or what on Earth will we do with all the leftover computer hardware and software? One organization in Portland, Oregon, has a terrific answer. Free Geek is a charity that takes donations of old computer stuff. Volunteers take the old equipment, refurbish it, install a free operating system, and make it Internet-ready—and the volunteers get a free computer after donating twenty-four hours of their time. Free Geek has taken over 700 tons of discarded computer stuff and assembled 4,000 working computers, and given them away. The best part is that it doesn't cost to participate. Check out *www.freegeek.org*. There are many other recycling organizations across the country that would be happy to receive your unused parts—just look them up on the Internet or in your phone book!

"Computer components make up as much as 40 percent of the content of our landfills. Many of the ingredients needed to manufacture them are extremely poisonous (lead, for example). These toxins are now leaching into the soil and threatening the purity of our drinking water."—Free Geek founder, Oso

If you have working computer equipment—hardware or software—you no longer want, it might tug someone's heart on eBay like it does yours. Outdated but still functional computer equipment can also be given to places like Goodwill or the Salvation Army, or to a local church or charitable organization that has a use for it (if you do this you can even take it as a tax deduction!).

For cutting clutter *on* computers, see "Clutter-Free Computing" (page 152) and "Junk E-mail" (page 129).

Video/DVD/CD Clutter

Seeing is believing, so what could be smarter than sending that message, delivering that pitch, or preserving that state-of-the-company address by videotaping it. This is sound in theory, but not too impressive in practice. Most of us have a tougher time viewing a video than reading, mainly because we don't always have the right player handy. And we seem to have less time for tape viewing at the office than at home.

I rarely run behind, but I have a backlog on my desk right now of eight things to watch! The pile wouldn't be so high if we didn't think that videoing those in-house meetings, speeches, and events was such a neat and easy way to make a record of them. Ninety percent of such recordings are never edited, and gads, are they bad, between poor lighting, poor sound, and terrible composition. Who ever watches them? It takes two hours of suffering to get ten minutes of value.

Then there are those motivational rah-rah tapes that didn't inspire us much the first time, the training tapes for the phone system we had before this one, DVDs with clips of two or three different uninteresting things on them, and the beta tapes we couldn't watch if we wanted to.

After you weed and erase these down to the ones that really are worth keeping, be sure to label or somehow otherwise identify the contents plainly and in detail. Otherwise, every time you come across it, it'll just be "what's this?" and then for *sure* you'll never watch it.

Ugly Plants in the Office (the Greenhouse Defect)

From the day a plant arrives in an office, it can be downhill all the way. Office plants are often overexamined and underfed. We water them too much or forget to water them at all, and don't divide or prune or repot them when we should. They shed everywhere, grow tall and spindly, or into a giant, impenetrable thicket. They stop blooming, lose that lovely shape we bought them for, and in general become more of an eyesore than a decoration.

Then too, of course, we have fertilizer stains on the carpet, water stains on the wall and rust on the file cabinet, and pot hanger holes in the ceiling.

The fake plants stay good-looking longer and are less trouble to maintain, but companies lose millions of dollars a year from people gathering in groups to discuss whether or not they're real.

Limit or eliminate indoor greenery where you can. Get a nice lush landscape print for the wall or bring in fresh flowers every so often. You'll save time, money, clutter, and window-sill space (as well as citations from the Prevention of Cruelty to Plants Society).

How can you keep plants in the office a plus, if you must have them? Take care of them! And if you find you are too forgetful or if the plants are shared among a few cube-mates, find a plant lover in the group and ask that he or she take care of them. Letting a landscaping service take care of them is the best bet, if you can afford it.

Fancy Frills, Ribbons, and Bows

We've all gone through a period of passion for the "pretty" office or workspace. The elegance we saw in a book or movie, or on a visit to a fancy office somewhere, really stuck in our head. We imagined that lavish decor would improve our image, and so we dreamed of an office with fancy furniture, exotic woods, expensive art or antiques, Persian rugs, a built-in saltwater aquarium, maybe even a real waterfall on the way in. The kind of office where more attention is paid to what's on the walls than to the work that comes out.

All this is vanity if not vexation. If an office is built or furnished like a hotel lobby, it just begs to be used that way. People pop in and pin you down for time-passing and idle trivia exchange. And a luxurious office may give clients and customers the impression that expensive padding is more important than the product or service offered.

I see so many people trying to function in a stiff, elegant setting of crystal, rosewood, and glistening chrome. It may look lovely, but there's really no place to work or, for that matter, even the right atmosphere for rolling up your sleeves and working.

When it comes to where we *work,* ornate surroundings can actually detract from the task at hand. Those who really do business get down to business—I agree with the real movers and shakers who say that when it comes to setting, the bare basics are real beauty. Then you don't have to tend or fiddle around with frills; you can just dead center on your duty, clean and pure, with no commercials or breaks to brag about or explain your ornaments.

Too often when we think of our workspace, we don't focus on its *function.* Having a cube or an office of our own is a real milestone for most of us. And many of us still think that way. But an office or cube is just a place in which to perform our business operations, not a trophy or tally of our life. It's just a tool, and one that needs to be kept clean and sharp so that we can dig, cut, pound, stir, and lift all the things we need to in life. Having this valuable tool rusted and clogged with (or even buried in) clutter is pretty dumb, or more to the point, unproductive.

Sticky Situation

Post-it notes took over faster than any other office product. One day they were unheard of, the next day the supply cabinet was packed with them in every size and shape. They may cut down on correspondence clutter because there's not much room to write on them, but they stick to not only what you intended but everything else, including the wrong documents, the sides of the trash can, and the computer screens everyone is always gluing them to.

Bad Taste in the Office

You might get away with "I'm Available" or "Muffler Men Do It Under the Car" on a T-shirt or cap if you're a truck driver, but posters, plaques, signs, etc., in questionable taste in the office can be job suicide. Think hard about the message any words or pictures on display in your workspace are sending.

You certainly wouldn't put a TGIF sign over your desk, even if you were that eager to get off work come the end of the week. It's not wise to advertise the fact that you don't like your job.

Some things you might like to have in your office and think are a sign of big business can actually be offensive to others. Alcohol or drinking-related accessories are one good example. Alcohol has been a business and life destroyer. If you like it, fine, but keep it *outside* the office.

Sexual messages likewise may seem funny for a minute or two but they are offensive to most people and they can get you fired. Bust ashtrays or mugs with lewd, suggestive, or just plain dumb sayings on them aren't creative or impressive or even funny. I've met many people who seemed to have good taste and class and then you get to their office and there sits some silly gadget or gaudy souvenir that pees on your hand or drops its drawers for a dime. Toss out all those titillating little tidbits and forget about the whoopee cushion mentality around the office.

Cord Clutter

Just look around the average office. Everything has to be plugged in (many things in more than one place). So running in, out, around, in front of, behind, and under everything is a writhing mass of cords that can rapidly make the nicest workspace look ratty. And, once one snakes from your desk to a power source of any kind, six more (for power packs, phones, printers, sound, heat, etc.) will follow. Don't be fooled; all those cordless phones and other "cordless" gizmos have a cord somewhere, too—usually in the form of an ugly recharging unit or two to occupy further space.

We can't cut those cords, unfortunately, but we can shorten and simplify them and make them much safer:

● Replace any overlong cords with shorter ones (of the right type and quality, of course).

- If that's not possible, at least reel up all those feet and yards of slack in your cords and twist-tie them into a neat compact coil.
- Take a hard look at the whole setup of what's plugged in, where, and with how many extension cords, etc. Is there anything (such as equipment you're no longer using) that could simply be eliminated or some way things could be arranged more efficiently, yet safely?
- The right kind of "plug in" or power strip (check with office maintenance or your local electrician) can consolidate cords into one neat group instead of fourteen baby octopi going off in all directions.
- Neatly encasing them in cord holders or using cord retractors, or just bundling some of the cords together (a Velcro strip or zip tie is a neat way to do this) will do wonders for the appearance and ease of maintenance of an office.

We become blind to clutter, and the only way to see it is to take everything out of a room, drawer, file, or office and then choose what to put back. The rest is clutter!

Desktop Drawer

This is usually the most important drawer in the desk—the control panel, the toolbox for all the basic office functions. It's right under our nose, in our lap when any office action occurs; it's where we keep everything that cuts, measures, marks, corrects, attaches, calculates—nice and handy but out of sight, too.

The middle desk drawer gets handled ten to one over the other drawers, whether we need a pen, a cough drop, or a trinket for a visiting kid. So we especially don't want it to be cluttered.

Every so often, get a canister vac and blow out that drawer fuzz, those eraser particles and little circles from the paper punch, etc. (never vacuum in here or you'll hear good stuff going rattle-clank up the hose). And the next time some time-waster calls you, open the drawer quietly, dejunk it, and neatly assemble what's left.

If the wide-open spaces of the middle drawer seem to be encouraging clutter (by creating the impression you can drop any old thing in there), you might consider some organizer trays. But read about "junk bunkers" (see page 39) first.

Once you have the middle drawer denuded it'll be a real inspiration for the rest of the place.

Low-Priority Things in High-Priority Space

Next in our decluttering campaign we need to deal with the worthwhile things we don't really use very often. Why crowd the glove compartment with jumper cables that ought to be in the trunk?

Right now you have, right on the front lines of your daily business battleground, lots of support material and other things that should be back in camp, in storage. I'm talking about things like old, but not obsolete, files and records, visual aids and displays, extra letterhead and other office supplies. Much of this is worth having and it can and will be used, or needs to be kept for reference. But you don't need it now, or you only need to refer to it once in a great while.

You've probably run across stuff in your desk, for example, that you haven't used for three years or more. It's not something you want to get rid of, but every time you reach into your desk, it's in the way or has to be moved, cleaned, or explained—those old check registers or the last address book you had before the one you're using now, for instance. You may need things like this once or twice in the next two years, but they sure don't have to be taking up room right on the desk.

We all have pictures and posters, too, that someday when we find a place, we are going to put up. If you keep these in your active working area, you know what they're going to look like by the time you can finally afford the framing job. Put them somewhere safe from damage as well as out of your way.

Storage Areas

Interesting how most of us think that if we had more storage we'd be better organized (just like "we'd be happier if we had more money"). Neatness isn't usually an issue of how much room we have—a good producer in even the most complex business can work out of a van or a suitcase instead of his or her usual office and keep it perfectly neat and functional all the while. And what happens when a company gets a bigger storage room? Do you see any improvement in the actual working areas? Not a bit. But there is something new in the brand-new storeroom: tons more old and inactive office junk, which mysteriously appears from everywhere!

Some storage rooms appear calm and even functional on the surface, but right underneath, right beyond those neatly stacked boxes of fifth and sixth copies of every letter anyone in the organization ever sent, is chaos. Here is every-thing we didn't want in our workspace because it was worn, broken, old, ugly, injured, outdated, or unneeded. Instead of getting rid of it there and then, we put it in storage to age for a while first. The first question to always ask yourself about storage is not *"where"* but *"why* should I be storing this at all?"

More room seldom relieves office congestion. The key is simply **LESS STUFF.** A bigger desk or office, more shelves, additional cabinets and credenzas generally just means more and bigger clutter.

"I thought I needed a new, larger filing cabinet, but all
I really needed was some creative self-discipline."

Storage Smarts

In more than fifty years of storing things and cleaning storage
areas (yours and mine), I've learned a few things I'd like to
share with you.

First off, you may know the wheat from the chaff, but
don't assume that everyone does. Unfortunately it often takes
a storage disaster to inspire us to reposition stuff before it
comes to ruin. Office people often take boxes of their good
records, etc., and just set them any old place.

One evening, my cleaning team walked into the janitor
closet of the city's main telephone building and there were
seven or eight boxes of old ticket-looking things. The boxes
weren't sealed, so we assumed they were trash and dumped
them. The next morning, the traffic department started
asking where all the records and billings for the long-distance
calls for the month were. Thanks to us, the entire city enjoyed
a lower phone bill that month.

In another building, a bank we cleaned, the manager
had tossed all the checks, etc., that came in that day into a
big cardboard box and was carrying it down to the computer
room after hours. While he scooted into the restroom, he set
the box down on top of the janitor's cart. The janitor, who
came along right behind him, carried them to the shredding
room and shredded the entire day's transactions. They hired
seventeen students for weeks to reconstruct the records.

Another time, we threw out a $42,000 set of original archi-
tectural drawings, a true disaster. Was it our fault or theirs?
The cleverest place to store "plans" in those days seemed to be
a shiny new thirty-gallon garbage can!

Remember—we're janitors, not mind readers. Some other things to remember:

Where and how you store things is important, as you've just learned.

Get it off the floor. Always store things up on either a skid or pallet or blocks or some four-by-fours, anything to get the bottom away from contact with the floor. Sooner or later, there'll be a flood, a spill, or some kind of moisture seepage on the floor, and it won't do anything good for those books or tax files in the bottom box. Boxes and containers sitting on the floor in an office have a short lifespan, as either water is going to flow under them when the janitors clean the floors, or the vacuum is going to beat them to death.

Repackage it. Don't just store things in what they came in. Repackage them if necessary, not only to protect them better but to make them more usable, findable, and stackable.

Go for first-class containers. Make sure it's sturdy if you want it to hold up in storage. Rubbermaid has performed a latter-day miracle for us storers. They make strong, good-looking, inexpensive plastic, stackable bins in all sizes. You just fill them—one, two, three, or thirty-three of them—neatly with the stuff you need to keep and then stack them. And instead of a half-acre site covered with disintegrating cardboard boxes, you can go all the way to the ceiling if you need to, and store thirty-two cubic feet of material on four square feet of floor space!

Mark all sides of each container with the contents. If you find the one you think you want at the bottom of a thirteen-foot stack, you can find out what's in it without renting a forklift.

Make dejunking easy. A nice big waste container in your storage area will help it stay clean.

Light: always have plenty of it in storage areas. It encourages neatness.

Chapter 5
Now for That Big Bad Backlog (of Paper)...

No matter how much of it there is, you have only two choices—do something, or don't do anything and suffer on. All those old notes and papers from "way back when" aren't so much a time problem (whether you'll admit it or not, you have the time) or a physical problem (it could be used for better things, but you do have the space; you can always find a corner). They're an emotional problem, a deep inner dread of having to face all those decisions. The worst weight of paper is the brain weight!

This is a disease with a cure, an easy, inexpensive, and rewarding one. We're going to dig it all out and sort it out.

Yes, You Are Going to Sort It

To build a model low-maintenance house, my wife and I bought four acres on Kauai, Hawaii. It truly was a jungle—trees, vines, and bushes so thick and dense and crammed together it was hard to even penetrate to the middle of the property to see what was there. Many of us have let our office backlog grow to the same condition—a solid mass of piles and stacks of paper—intimidating and overwhelming, with no clear place to start. So we put it off for months, years, decades, even.

True, there is plenty of old, obsolete, and ruined stuff there (dead branches, rotten logs, and fallen leaves), but there is some gold in there somewhere too. So we can't just scoop it all up and dump it. People do reach the point of total disgust or find they have to make an emergency move, and they end up just loading the whole pile and hauling it to the trash, without ever examining it. Or they take it to one of those little self-storage mausoleums to rot, which is pretty much the same thing.

Remember, there are worthwhile things in there, so always cut through the mounds carefully. NEVER dump without doing some selection, no matter how mean and desperate you feel—it will haunt you forever and you'll lose some good stuff.

For our Hawaii jungle, we brought sharp knives, a couple of treasure boxes, and a big container for trash and carefully began whittling away at the edge of the jungle. And indeed, we found valuable plants and special trees and pretty stones that we wanted to save. The same thing will be true of your backlog—cutting through it will bring you not only peace of mind, but also some neat things you didn't expect and some pleasant surprises.

There's no other way to beat backlog than to swing a sharp knife or sickle and create a large trash pile as you go. Prayer and fasting, bigger compactors, or a reprimanding boss won't do it. The only two words needed here are *you* and *now*.

Dumb Pieces of Paper We All Keep

- Claim forms for insurance companies we are no longer with
- Insurance receipts for packages that were delivered
- Bankbooks from defunct accounts
- The "bottom half" (stubs) of checks issued by businesses—even when nothing is written or typed on there ("if it was attached to/associated with a check, it must be important")
- Loser lottery tickets, expired coupons
- Leases to places we moved out of a decade ago
- Anything more than two copies of each of your previous resumes
- Forms (such as expense report forms) from past jobs
- Receipts for minor amounts we forgot to include in past tax returns
- Empty postage stamp books
- Business cards from salespeople we never want to see again
- "This product was packed/inspected by" slips

It'll Go Faster Than You Think

Let me make it a little easier for you to get at it now: It isn't going to take as long as you think. Even if you have rooms full of old papers, often what you expected to take weeks or months will end up more like days. In a couple of days we had a place for our house and yard cleared in the jungle—it looked like a two-month job, but it was done in two days.

Remember, the older the paper, the faster you can usually shear through it (because you're a long way now from the hopes, fears, and illusions that caused you to keep most of it in the first place). Just think, something you've dreaded and been depressed by all this time, even been ribbed or ridiculed for, could be relieved in forty-eight hours. Or surely with just a few days of full-time work, or a week or so of every spare minute. It's amazing how fast a backlog melts away when you stick with it, not just moan about it and peck away at it.

We all have trouble persuading ourselves to tackle a teetering pile of papers—it might help to previsualize, before you start, the relief, pleasure, or confidence all that clear space is going to bring!

A Formula to Help You Face It

Here's a formula that will help you deal more efficiently with those piles of papers when you do open the door and reach into them. You need four sturdy boxes, a pair of scissors, a stapler, a staple remover, a permanent marker, tape, a trash can, and a pencil or pen and paper for notes (some nice, fresh new ones!).

Label your first box OUT. This is an easy one, because much of that stuff that's been lying around all this time is defunct or defiled or outdated or too late to do anything about, and even you, the savior of any old morsel from a magazine, won't want it and will find it easy to eliminate for good. This is at least 50 percent of the piles, and there's nothing to it. A giant chunk of it is now gone in only the time it takes you to glance at it quickly, confirm that it's true clutter, and cast it. (Actually, you might want to line up a giant trash barrel for this category.)

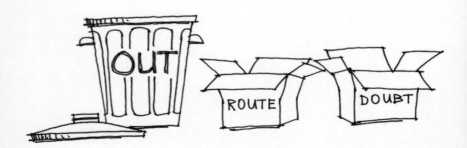

Label the second box ROUTE. Into this second box goes the worthwhile stuff that belongs somewhere else or to someone else. Toss all this into the Route box and when you're done, pick up that whole boxful and put or send everything back where it belongs. Or stick a note, address, or shipping label on each thing that tells where or to whom it goes, and have someone else disperse it all.

(By now this is actually getting to be fun, because you're finding neat stuff you kept and forgot all about. Some fine stuff that was buried alive has been revived and reactivated, and you're really getting motivated now. Especially when you think of all the *room* you're going to have soon. . . .)

The third box should be labeled DOUBT. You might still want or need it, but you're not 100 percent sure what it is, or you want to check on it further. Drop this stuff into the Doubt box. But know that the unbendable rule of this box is that you work on it every single day (carry it around with you, if you must) until all the doubts are resolved and it's E-M-P-T-Y, right down to the bare cardboard.

Label the last box SPROUT. Into it goes the good business-related stuff you really wanted and are ready to use at last. This is the high-grade ore, the notes and ideas that could change the world (or at least your job or company), the addresses and leads and sources and real keeper info that you really needed, those long-lost warranties and instructions, etc. Whatever you do, remember you really have to activate or file this stuff now, not just repile it!

The "Quick Weight Loss" Approach

Another technique that helps combat the discouraging aspect of paper clutter is to go through the mass really fast, tossing all that can be tossed immediately and putting the rest into boxes or piles of things that do seem to need consideration or at least a closer look. This helps because it immediately reduces the mass that must be gone through. Taking a real look at three or even thirteen boxes of stuff is a lot less demoralizing than a whole roomful. The older the paper stash, the better this works. We can see the idiocy of a lot of stashed paper stuff more quickly and clearly when it's fifteen or twenty or even a half-dozen years old.

The secret then, of course, is to circle back and slash through, not restash, those remaining boxes.

You Don't Have to Be in the Office to Declutter

When we're there, in fact, we're generally so bombarded with calls and visitors and e-mails we have very little time to deal with backlog. So take some of that aged paper out with you—even if the pile is a foot or two high and the box you put it in needs sideboards, take it away from the office with you. Then, over the weekend or in the evening at home you can look it over, sort it, evaluate it, deal with it. In one day you'll get through more clutter and "To Do Someday" stuff than in a full week at the office. You can shear through office overload anywhere, regardless of noises or distractions. Wind is about the only liability, and sometimes that can even help your decisions by blowing away some of the lighter stuff! Seriously, though, give it all a fair shake before you shake it off.

What about That Unopened Mail? . . .

This is a sin most of us have committed sometime—almost every home or office I've ever cleaned had a little cache somewhere of unopened mail.

The fact that we've never gotten around to this has nothing to do with time, as we may have told ourselves—it's all a matter of mood. We didn't open it because we're afraid it's bad news, something unsettling, more work or problems to be dealt with when we have more than enough already. So we convince ourselves that as long as it's left sealed and unread we stay free. But exactly the opposite is true—unopened mail multiplies not only problems, but also mental anguish. (Besides, you could be wrong; it could be a check or a credit or congratulations. I know you think you have return-address-scanning down to a science, but you could be way off.) I guarantee you that at least 70 percent of the time that envelope contains something far more harmless than you thought. And at least another 10 percent will be harmful but too old to do much about now anyway.

So unearth those unopened business-related envelopes and the minute one of the following moods strikes, grab that letter opener and get to it:

1. I don't care anymore, nothing matters.
2. I'm flying too high to be shot down.

If waiting even one more minute suddenly seems silly to you, good! Open them right now and RIGHT THIS MINUTE do whatever you have to do to make amends: call, write, thank, send that check or overdue present. DON'T get hung up on the length and magnificence of the apology that seems called for; save all your strength for the actual doing of whatever has to be done. Then resolve to never leave anymore little "time bombs" in heaps.

The following table shows the official guidelines for procrastinators (found on an office wall in Ohio).

Aging Guide for All Forms of Speedy Mail

Type	To Do
FedEx, Purolator, Airborne, and other courier services, and U.S. Postal Service Express Mail	Let sit for one day, or at least the afternoon of the day received.
Certified mail	It's probably something bad/we don't want to know; never open it.
Certified mail, return receipt requested	Leave it at the post office for at least fifteen days, and it'll go away automatically (Uncle Sam won't hold it any longer than that).
UPS next- and second-day air	It could easily be confused with the pile of unopened regular UPS in the corner.
Priority mail	It's a little less expensive and visible, so we can fib or fudge about what day we actually received it.
Mailgrams and cables	It's so unusual, we could be excused for spending a few days pondering the novelty/audacity of it.
Carrier pigeon	Oops—who let the cat out?!
Pony Express	After eight days in the saddle, what's one more day?
Hand-delivered by personal messenger	Only accept if he's also carrying a pizza.
E-mail and other forms of fast computer mail	Not everyone turns on the computer every single day, after all.
Voice mail	Gosh, I guess my mailbox was full.
Fax	After all that time spent getting it to go through, and at least two long-distance calls confirming that it was received or sent, who has time to actually read it?
Wire transfers	We can always use the excuse the banks do: These things take time to be registered in the system.

Do a Good Deed as You Dejunk: Paper Recycling

Big decluttering binges or just keeping the daily paper stream weeded down means plenty of wastepaper. Over half the waste from a typical office is high-grade recyclable paper. So recycle! Yes, it does mean a little extra sorting and separating and a little extra wielding of the staple remover, but it's nice to know that at least some of that excess paper is going back to good use.

Paper recycling is available almost everywhere, with a promise of greater efficiency and convenience to come. Jump on the recycling bandwagon right now—this is a worthwhile effort for every one of us, not just the office next door.

Do bear in mind that if your recycling campaign isn't set up intelligently, it can actually *add* to office clutter, with a bunch of bins, cans, boxes, and schedules around that no one even remembers to use.

Educating everyone in the effort is probably the most critical part. AT&T, for example, once hired me to come to one of their New York offices and write some production procedures for the company. While I was there, one of

Cycling Through Paper

Recycling helps keep everyone aware of the sheer volume of junk paper, too. How much paper do we clutterers use? More than 187 billion pounds of paper a year, in this country alone. If that doesn't make much of an impression on you, that many pounds of paper, if it were 8½" × 11"−sized sheets, would be 18.7 trillion sheets, 81,000 of them gone through just by you alone in a year.

• • • • • • • •

the higher-ups went to a recycling seminar and came back enthused. He ordered a sharp little paper-recycling center for every desk in the building. They arrived on Friday, and on Saturday, while we maintenance people were in there working and everyone else was gone, the executive had the janitors place a little unit on each desk. Monday morning arrived, and everyone was delighted with their surprise new "desk organizer," and quickly put it to use in their daily paper processing: one slot for important active documents, one for pending, one for things that needed to be refiled, etc. No one had informed the office workers that these were recycling trays, but the janitors had been so instructed, and that night they efficiently emptied the contents of all the trays into the shredding bins.

The next morning the place was in chaos. Scores of contracts and other important documents, including checks and letters, were gone, gone, gone!

Paper recycling is important, and it's here to stay, and it's like the day they finally tell us we need glasses to see better. We need to quit fighting it and figuring ways around it, and just find a way to do it—neatly, efficiently, and well.

P.S. Clean Off the Clutter Ring, Too

As soon as you dejunk your workspace, clean off the clutter "ring." A decluttered office will have its high-water marks—nail holes, lean marks, and scuffs on the walls, rust stains on the floors, impressions where something sat for so long, dust and debris left behind by disposed-of boxes, cup rings on the blotter or desk, etc. If these aren't removed too, everyone will remember the chaos that once was your workspace!

Chapter 6

Those All-Too-Cluttered "Common Areas"

In most offices there's a kind of "no man's land" that's listed in professional cleaners' contracts as "the public areas." You know these well and use them as much as your own personal space. I'm talking about places like the halls, cafeteria or lounge room, locker room, the mail/utility room, conference rooms, the backroom (storage), and the parking area.

We treat these areas kind of the way many people treat the public roadside. In our own front yard we pick up wrappers and blown newspapers, and even the cans that someone else throws there, but on the median and roadsides in general, anything goes and everything goes out the window. Consider the *conference room,* for example. We pro cleaners call this "the massage parlor of paper," because it has no real storage or staging place for paper, yet everyone brings plenty of it in there, and spends plenty of time massaging it. And bored and preoccupied folks not only spread it all out, but they also leave it behind. The thoughts that contribute to conference room clutter run something like this:

> *"Ah, this place is so big and roomy, it's a shame to leave it empty and unused."*
>
> *"If I leave something open with a pen by it, it'll look so official no one will touch it."*
>
> *"If I leave that stuff on the whiteboard, it'll impress the boss when she comes ambling by, or maybe even the janitors when they erase it."*
>
> *"As for these unhanded-out handouts, after all that work putting them together they deserve to live a few days longer. Eventually someone will realize they're obsolete and throw them out."*
>
> *"I'll just leave my candy wrappers, empty coffee cups, and crumpled papers right here, instead of dragging them back to my office."*

You better have a conference with your conscience!

So Many Rooms to Fill, So Little Time

Each of the public office spaces seems to invite certain clutter, like lobbies, another good place to leave and forget things or sit for a long time and fidget and wait. In lobbies, we doodle, make notes, contort paper clips, scatter magazines, and in general, disorganize and litter up the place, because we're bored or nervous.

We all leave stuff in the *cafeteria* or *lunchroom,* too. It seems so logical to leave cups and mugs and unwashed plastic containers around, cans and jars of our special diet foods, and microwave utensils and accessories. Not to mention all those plastic forks and knives and straws and the containers the supermarket salad bar delicacies came in.

The cold facts are that the *company/communal refrigerator* is the oldest, ugliest mess in the office public area. Everyone leaves partly consumed things there, and since it's cold in there, we somehow assume they'll last forever. Plus, everyone is reluctant to throw out anyone else's stuff. So no one tosses *anything* out, and there's no room to put anything. The refrigerator is just a moldy cave of Styrofoam cups and containers half-filled with soups and "Slimfeast" concoctions, plates of partly eaten sandwiches complete with now gruesome garnishes, stale muffins, rock-hard bagels, almost empty bottles of sour milk or flat soda, disemboweled pies, shriveled pizza from the last company luncheon, rotting bananas and apples, outdated medications, and brown paper bags no one even wants to open.

Are you among those who contribute more than your share to the shameful condition of the refrigerator? If so, then get with it and get it out . . . and keep it out. You might want to go to enforced refrigerator emptying, as many offices have. "The refrigerator is cleaned out the last Friday of the month and anything unclaimed will be disposed of!"

Halls remind me of a doorstep where someone anonymously leaves a basket and makes a run for it. You office folk drive the custodians crazy with all the stuff you just happened to lean, set, or store in the hall. As if it were just going to disappear to some designated distant home. The "forgotten" rate for anything halled is phenomenal, and in fact, most of us who set things in the hall are actually hoping (if not praying) that someone will make off with it.

Coat closets are mini-tombs of a sort, a place to leave things we aren't sure are worth keeping: broken umbrellas, ratty old raincoats, single gloves, poorly crocheted scarves, battered hats, anonymous shopping bags, topless Tupperware, burned-out light bulbs, old signs, and the plastic-domed tray the cold cuts for the last office party came in (surely it could be used for something!).

Some of us have **lockers** at work to keep tools, towels, work clothes, safety equipment, and such handy when we need them. And it would really be convenient, too, if the average locker wasn't such a compressed cylinder of clutter.

The *utility room* is the resting place where you can usually find any excess we did divest ourselves of—still not hauled away.

As for the *copy area:* Once that magnificent machine has done what we wanted, we take the treasure (those nice sharp copies) and leave the original (at least ⅓ of the time) and all those ruined, too-light, or crooked copies. Plus the misfed paper, trimmings from any paper cutting we did, the packaging from anything we unwrapped, the empty toner cartridges, and at least two dozen paper clips, staples, or dispossessed Post-it notes.

(And if the machine breaks or runs out of paper, we leave it that way!)

The medicine cabinet in the bathroom at home and the *supply cabinet* at work both have one really bad strike against them. Multiple users! Anytime more than one person puts things into or removes things from storage you have big problems. Everyone uses the cabinet but no one is responsible for it, so it ends up both jumbled and overloaded—full of old, half-used inks and toners, wrinkled warranties, torn-off shrink-wrap, obsolete letterhead, tops to stationery boxes, warped rolls of tape, shelf-worn self-stick labels, and odd-sized or odd-colored anything. Once it reaches this condition, it encourages us to use it as a dropping place for broken parts, old and torn typewriter covers, and first-aid kits with all the important stuff missing. Eventually it's just a vertical junk drawer.

The solution to all this pollution is to (some dark night or early morning) take it upon yourself to shake it down secretly. Okay, it may be "theirs" or "ours," but it's a great warm-up for getting at yours later. And it's always easier—even irresistible!—to declutter someone else's stuff! Never say a word about it after you do it, and everyone will think someone else did it. It works every time.

The **back room** gets everything we dismissed from, or don't need in, the office. It isn't really worth either dragging home or keeping, so we store it in the backroom awhile: broken coffeepots and fans, ugly picture frames, unclaimed coats, half-congealed cans of paint, partial badminton sets, rusty old trunks, three-legged tables, uncomfortable old couches, tables with ruined tops, and boxes of never-decided-what-to-do-with-it paperwork. About now you are saying "But I hardly have anything back there . . . or maybe only one or two things—how could that hurt?" You may be right, but if there are thirty of you in your office and you each leave only 3 things a month there, that's 90 a month, more than 1,000 a year.

Restrooms have clutter, too—newspapers, magazines, and other abandoned reading material, and all kinds of grooming accessories from hairpins, combs, and brushes to hairdryers and compacts. (If there's a closet or lounge by the restroom, it's filled with clothes clutter—see page 58.)

Parking Area

In my cleaning seminars, I always offer a prize for the right answer to the following question: "What is the first place the public sees in our office buildings?" The guesses range from "the lobby" to "the restrooms" to "the elevators," but seldom does anyone guess it. The answer we've all over-looked: the parking lot. Yes, as we walk or drive in to do business somewhere, this is the first thing we all notice, and from which we draw our conclusions about the neatness and cleanliness of a place. And you know how the lot looks after a few people decide to dump their ashtrays here, and then a few more clean out their front seats, divesting them-selves of their empty cups and cans and bags, their drop-pings and drippings and crumpled wrappers. Wonder who owns those cars?

Your clutter contribution to public areas should be zero—nothing. The rule for public office areas, like the rule for public recreation areas, should be: What you bringeth, you taketh away.

People who would never tape an ugly announcement poster up on the wall of their own office will do it in a public place without a second's hesitation. I'm not trying to slap your wrist, just to raise your consciousness a little when it comes to public places. Even when you have a lab partner, share a joint desk, or do a group project, *you* are still individually respon-sible for cleaning it up if it gets messed up.

Ever See a Custodian Cry? (The Janitor Closet)

I'm always amazed at how many of you dump and store your stuff in our janitor closets. Already they build or give us the tiniest rooms in the place . . . to do one of the biggest jobs. And unless we lock and bolt it, we'll arrive to find a selection of office offal like you wouldn't believe packed in there. We can handle people borrowing some of our tools, or even swiping a spray bottle or two, but not leaving broken chairs, bedraggled holiday decorations, retired typewriters, dead plants, and the stuff no one cared enough about to claim in the last ten years from the lost and found.

Even in public places and corporate settings, your stuff is yours!

The Clutter Cast and Crew

You might want to meet some of the characters who contribute mightily to common-area clutter (and compound cleaning costs):

Gretchen Groomer leaves grooming residue all over as she combs her hair, applies nail polish, and files her nails every-where and anywhere. Beautifying should be done at home or discreetly in the restroom.

Ed Borrower (and return in wrong place)—what's his is his, and what's yours is "ours." Helping himself to things with or without permission is bad enough, but the fact that he never returns anything to the right place makes him a disaster.

Gertie Gumjaw doesn't just chew gum, she sticks it under tables and desks, drops it on the sidewalk and parking lot, and abandons it at the water fountain. No matter where it ends up, it looks awful and quadruples cleaning time.

Tossing Thomas is an NBA reject; he misses every time and he doesn't follow through. All bad shots should be rebounded into the receptacle.

Ned Nibbles leaves crumbs and wrappers everywhere, and his stash attracts roaches and rodents and creates stains and spills. Food and drink should be confined to eating areas.

Homefront Hannah—it's not only impossible to clean around her collection of homey clutter, it's an eyesore. And it's all too easy to bump and break her treasures.

Teresa Tapewall ruins walls and other surfaces with tape, glue, tacks, and other stickums. It leaves an unsightly mess behind, and most adhesives are not easily removable, if they even can be removed. Posters and announcements should be put on the bulletin board.

Sidney Spillage is always nursing a cup of something, as he sits at his desk or jogs down the hall. He leaves drips and rings everywhere and thinks nothing of throwing half-full cups into the trash can. His leaks and spills cause lots of stains.

Stacey Stapletoss seems to delight in dropping staples, paper clips, and thumbtacks all over the floor, where they get embedded in the carpet and have to be pried out. All this loose hardware clogs and breaks vacuums, too.

Stan Scatterpack—the minute he rips open any mail, the wrappers, strings, tape, and Styrofoam peanuts of any package are scattered and ignored.

Frank Feetonwall (and on desks, tables, and other furniture).

Vic Vendor leaves snack fallout, cups, and wrappers everywhere and makes it possible for candies, mints, and cheese-coated popcorn to be crushed into the floor. The vending machine area is an extra-good place to pick up after yourself.

J. P. Stallseat Journal always leaves behind the latest edition, and it gets tromped on and spread all over—which means litter and ink tracked everywhere. (It takes the janitors longer to scrape up the disintegrating paper than to clean the stalls.)

Hank and Harriet Heels get black marks and spike heel punctures all over, and you can just about forget the floor right under their desks.

Grady Graffiti and Violet Vandal like to leave their mark. After they visit our parks and forests (carving their names, drawing, painting, and marking) they come to work and deface the place. They write on stalls and walls (even in the tile grout), pick at and chip paint, shred fabric, and leave pen marks on every available surface.

Edgar Ignore sees something that's broken (or about to be), or a dangerous spill, litter, or even a vandal, yet he won't pick it up, fix it, or take a minute to tell someone else about it.

A much appreciated code of office conduct: Pick up what you drop!

The Curse of the Common Areas: Coffee Clutter

Nothing looks worse or soils and slows up a desk and office like coffee clutter. Most office inhabitants have not one cup or mug (for this habit they want to shake), but three. And even if there isn't a percolator or drip machine and all the trappings cuddled in some corner, there are the spoons and stirrers and napkins, and sugars and creamers real and artificial, stuck in every conceivable place to be punctured and sifted and drifted all over the place. Not to mention the drips and stains and spills all over not only the desktop and your clothes and the carpet, but also on papers that were supposed to be kept pristine. And the more cups of coffee, the more trips to the restroom. If you cut coffee out of your office, think how much time and mess and distraction you'd save.

Coffee (tea, chicken bouillon), of course, isn't the only offender here. I've heard from some readers:

"A soda was knocked over onto an important document with six different signatures. The document had to be redone and sent back to all those people to be resigned."

"A soft drink overturned on a desk and ruined an elaborate set of ledger cards, which had to be re-created."

"Back in the dark ages before computers and even before memory typewriters, a legal secretary had finished a long document that had to be filed that day. Her desk was cluttered with drafts, papers, pens, and the document. She reached to answer the phone, knocked her cola over, and ruined the original. I don't remember if the court deadline was ever met, but I never again kept a cup of anything in the work path. I'm glad I learned the lesson from someone else."

Drinks right at your desk are really risky, whether you work with plain old, easily ruined paper or a computer. Abstinence is a sure cure, but if your coffee and cola needs are uncontrollable, at least be careful. Keep all beverages well out of the way of either phones or computers. For *any* office imbibing, the safest approach is to *never* set any liquid on the same surface as your work itself—set it on an entirely separate piece of furniture, or even the floor if there's no other alternative. And when you're finished with a cup of something but it is not empty, don't just abandon it any old place or put it in the wastebasket. If all 30 or 300 or 3,000 people in your office just toss a third of a cup of something in the trash each day, that's gallons of liquid in formerly dry trash. Where does it go? What does it do? It rusts containers and creates ugly stains and odors, as well as lots of additional need for cleaning.

Dump Those Candy Dishes

They look tacky, take up prime space, generate dropped wrappers, and contribute not just to tooth decay and office vermin populations but to the annoying sounds of people slurping and crunching all around the place.

Janitors hate candy dishes, and not only because they're always being accused of eating someone's cinnamon bears. They know that after anyone tries a piece of candy they don't like, the half-chewed remains will be laid quietly on a windowsill or dumped in the wastebasket to stick to the sides.

Horticultural Horrors

Plant enthusiasts are notorious trespassers on the common ground. They introduce one pot and we end up with a forest or a jungle, vines crawling all over the place. Add to this all those partially used bags of potting soil and emptied pots and miniature trellises and landscaping tools that have to go somewhere, too. . . . Ever see anyone take them home? Nope. They're stashed in the storage or utility room, or in the janitor closet!

A Critical Rule for Common Areas: Put It Right Back!

How many times have parents told their kids, "Well, if you'd put it back where it belonged, you could find it." At least 80 billion.

No greater truth of object management has been so often spoken, or so little heeded. How easy it is to put something away or back where it goes right when we're done with it. It's usually just a matter of seconds, yet we won't do it. Then we'll spend minutes, even hours or days, trying to dig it out or locate it when we need it again.

Nowhere is the Put It Right Back rule more important than in the office, because it usually has multiple users of tools and machines. Just listen, and you'll hear the cries of consternation and inefficiency from every direction:

- Has anyone seen the big stapler?
- Who has the paper cutter?
- Where's the key to the washroom/storeroom?
- Who used the packing tape last?
- Who took the telephone book?
- Where is the projector?
- Gasp! I left that tape in the VCR. . . . Where did it go?
- What happened to the instruction manual?
- Don't we have a dustpan?
- Where's just one of the thirteen pairs of scissors we own?

Pathetic, isn't it? And who pays? You! A file drawer is left out after the single thing someone was looking for is found, and someone tips it over. Now it's a major mess that takes hours to put back in order.

This isn't a group failing, it's an individual failing. Crews and committees don't carry things away or leave them out—it's you . . . *you*. You do it to others and you do it to yourself and others do it to you. It always irritates and costs plenty, in cold cash as well as time lost. Here's one resolution for the New Year that will save you, the office, and the home scene, too, a lot of grief. Put things back as soon as you are through with them! One way to help this happen is to have storage places well marked and convenient. If that doesn't work, try a little chain on the item like the bank puts on its pens!

Don't Invade Anyone Else's Chaos

A little caution here now before we go any further.

No matter how disorderly someone else's desk is, no matter how long it festers in your organized mind, no matter how bad it looks or how much it eggs you on, or how many ugly shadows it casts on your neat desk, **don't try to organize or dejunk anyone else's desk or workspace.** Not even your very own assistant's (if you're lucky enough to have one). Even landfills have boundaries and plunder rules. You just can't invade someone else's chaos. It isn't ethical or friendly, and it will put any relationship you have with him or her immediately into the past tense.

All you can do is give a good example, offer assistance in an unobnoxious way, or leave a few empty garbage containers handy for them to use.

Decluttering is like weight loss or exercise—you can't talk other people into it or do it for them. *They* have to decide to do it, and then do it of their own free choice and will. You're dealing with the most intense and primordial of instincts here—"possession" and "territory"—as you will discover if you ignore what I'm telling you!

Chapter 7

The Clutter You Can't See . . . Mental Clutter

Remember back to all the places you've been in your life, Golden Gate to Gettysburg, Yellowstone to Yankee Stadium, Grandma's house to the White House—how they made you feel superseded all other impressions taken into your soul. We've all walked into mansions and felt cold, walked into tacky tract housing and felt warmth and love. It's the same with people. People can have all the brains, power, and money in the world, and yet leave you empty and unsettled. Others in contact with us for only minutes can project a feeling of peace and serenity we'll never forget.

Most of us have thought, even worried, about the aura within the walls of our home, but have you ever considered the feeling your office or workspace gives? After all, this is where a large portion of your life is spent and some of your most important friends and allies originate. You can clean up the place, get rid of every last excess photocopy and empty cardboard box, yet it can still be cluttered. With something you can't see or touch, maybe, but unquestionably can feel. Shall we single out some of it, this invisible stuff that crowds and chokes out and offends, and call it intangible or *mental clutter*?

Maybe we should include it on our list of toss-outs.

Politics and Cliques

Surely office politics are uglier than an old mildewed box of receipts—power-playing at the office: playing up to people, playing favorites, trading favors, focusing all your attention on "advantages" and stepping stones, spending all your time documenting things instead of just doing them and letting them speak for themselves.

After 1,500 books and 2,000 coffee break conferences, all advising you that office politics are a vital part of the business world, I'm here to tell you that all of that is office clutter. Remember, in politics you always have to worry about keeping all your campaign promises, those obligations to give and receive—and talk about clutter. WOW! Blowing smoke can easily consume 90 percent of our time and energy, and leave us very little time to light any real fires in what we do.

Bureaucracy

Red tape . . . rituals . . . forms and forms and multiple copies. Orderly, proper, and polite procedures are as good an idea in office work as anywhere, but too much of this sort of thing is

clutter in capital letters. It's bad news when you find yourself spending more time keeping track than making tracks. Butt-covering takes a lot of time and creates a lot of clutter, and it always gets in the way of real work. A pity, isn't it, that some situations seem to reward people just for the volume of time used and stuff generated, regardless of its content. Bureaucracy only builds office clutter, not character.

Office Parties and Affairs

Romantic entanglements breed nothing but long-range heart-break for all concerned. At the office we see each other at our best dressed and best behaved, our most attractive presentation of ourselves. There are no hair curlers or babies crying, and our little weaknesses of personal finance or personal hygiene are much less apparent. We're kind of an edited edition of our-selves. So, naturally, many people are attracted to each other, and the resulting footsie-playing and hanky-panky can and does create and perpetuate a big unseen mess in the office.

Offices have enough tendencies toward trouble without including that powder keg called romantic emotion. It's hard enough to concentrate on work in the face of more compelling urges, without having the object of our affection under the same roof, or in the same room.

Gossip

Our mouth can resemble our office drawers sometimes—jammed full of things that aren't needed and that don't do us or anyone any good. Gossip has undone more office efficiency than all the junk mail in this century. Gossip is like a bad virus, unseen but spreading steadily and insidiously. What it doesn't kill, it contaminates and alienates. Let it run rampant in your office and a messy desk will seem mild by comparison.

Complaining

Complaints are such a staple of office clutter that on a good day of heavy complaining you can almost feel them hanging in the air. You could define coffee break, for example, as an interval in which full-grown people huddle together and complain. They complain about their salaries, the weather, their working conditions, the boss, the supervisor, the vending machines, the cafeteria, the uniforms, the wallpaper, the janitors. They complain for so long the coffee gets cold and then they go into overtime and complain about that. Complaint (gossip, criticism, rumor-exchanging) breaks do more damage to a company's morale than can be imagined. If complaining in businesses stopped today, this country would double its productivity. We all know that problems won't stop coming, and if we just cut down on our complaining, we'll find a more than equal gain in our motivation and accomplishments.

What people don't like, they should change . . . or leave. Complaining all around the office is like pouring bad water in a good well. It'll mix in with and poison the progress, attitude, and enthusiasm of all. Now after almost fifty years as a boss and business owner, I can assure you that all complaints are recorded somewhere . . . to be repeated at the wrong time to the boss or someone in charge. When you toss out the rest of your old office stuff, toss out forever any habitual complaining. It's about the worst of the unseen office clutter.

Noise

Noise is a big unseen drug today. People are so used to it, so dependent on it to dull their senses and blot out other things, they can't seem to live without it. "I can't concentrate without noise" is the inane mouthing of a sound addict fooling himself. Kids claim they need noise to study by, and "white noise" is even released in open office complexes to override the noise of production.

The truth is that noise bothers 95 percent of us, offends 80 percent, and infuriates at least half. Radios, TVs, printers, phones, copy machines, people chitchatting or chewing loudly

or clinking or clanking things around the office are all unseen clutter. It makes clear, clean thinking almost impossible. If you are or own the cause of it, unplug or relocate it.

Odors in the Office

In days past this might have meant the bouquet of roses someone brought in, or the whisper of perfume or cologne. Today, the odors in the office are not only nose-testing but eye-smarting. They outdo those of my early life spent around sheep dip and cattle corrals. There's no more whispering—it screams. Even men "Brut" themselves with all kinds of perfumes and potions—after-shave, deodorant, toothpaste, mouthwash, hairspray, and even shoelaces are odor-doused. Then there are those leftovers from deli lunches kept at the desk for "later" or to take home—those heady spices are on her breath already, so the stasher can't smell them, but others can, and hate it.

To counteract all this we bring in odor killers, which is kind of like bringing the urinal block out of the men's room into the office. There are candles and potpourri of all kinds set all over in little dishes that not only smell up the place, but also get spilled and have to be cleaned around. Plain old clean air is so good and is now almost impossible to find in an office. Too much of even an exquisite scent is clutter and can be as big a turnoff to clients and coworkers as a pile of cowpies on your desk.

Hangers-On

We might be so unkind as to call these folks "live clutter." I'm talking about the people who are always there like a pile of mail waiting to be processed. Out West we call people like these "drifters," folks who blow in or through the office like a tumbleweed, catch somewhere, and stick. They have nothing to really do, say, or contribute and are generally too dumb to move on when you start working on something or pick up the phone. They do have good timing, however, for just when you're wondering when they're going to leave, they sit down again and ask, "How's everything else going?"

Leaving our space open to anybody who happens by is like having the drawers of our desk open with a sign that says "Set junk here." I don't even keep a chair in my office for visitors to sit on if they do drift in. Hangers-on hate to stand.

As for the hangers-on known as salespeople, don't let them snooker you into buying something just to get rid of them. Let them know when *you* want to see them (if there is actually some good reason to), and make it clear that the shorter their stay, the better you'll like them.

Talk about clutter. . . . If we could all just cut
out *interruptions*, we'd have one of the biggest
sources of mental clutter in the office whipped.

Meetings

Meetings can be defined as a place where we keep minutes and squander hours. Or as a time when you assemble others to hear what they have to contribute, hoping it won't conflict too much with what you've already decided on.

Most people already know before a meeting what they have or haven't done and what they should do. The only purpose of the meeting is to discuss the excuses or divide the blame. The most basic, simple happening can be made complicated or even unsolvable if enough meetings are held and enough people are invited to discuss it.

How often do we call or arrive somewhere to get something done and find the principals unavailable because they're "in a meeting." As if meetings were somehow sacred, immune to mundane everyday action. Meetings, in fact, are only an appendage to action! So much time can be spent in meetings, and in planning and lining up leaders, and arranging times and places for them, there is little ambition left for the actual doing. And consider all the energy everyone expends remembering and preparing for a meeting (rather than on the problem for which the meeting is being called).

I wonder how many meetings there'd be if, before we walked in, we had to hand over what they actually cost us, not only in terms of actual time lost, but in cold cash as well. Even totally worthless interoffice meetings can easily cost $800 to $1,000 in wages and snacks, and fly-in meetings can easily run up to $5,000 or far more. Much of this could be handled more efficiently over the phone, in a letter, or an e-mail exchange. The more I avoid meetings of any kind, the faster and more effective I become!

Junk Phone Calls

The telephone is a fantastic thing. The speed! The reach! The quality! The reasonable cost! What in history has helped communications like this instant transmittal of a voice over any distance, at any time of the day or night?

The telephone is so easy to use, too . . . and so overused. Even at home, too many calls and calls that are too long take our time and can irritate others who are trying to get through. But at work, the phone can be more of a burden than government documentation requirements.

The phone gives anyone an open invitation to invade, break in on anything, anytime. Phones actually rule many homes and offices, as if that ring were sacred. And because we're in business, that phone has to be there and operating all the time. We often get to the end of the day exhausted, yet discouraged because we accomplished nothing. As for why, we can count twenty phone calls, sixteen of which were twice as long as they needed to be, or totally unnecessary. Phones are often used to compensate for poor record-keeping and planning.

As callers we all hate screeners, but as receivers of calls, we'd all like the best "phone filter" we can find. Yet some of the very devices we install in hopes of cutting down phone clutter end up adding to the wasted time and expense in the end—such as answering machines and voice mail. I'd rather get no answer than leave a message and still not know when and if I'll get an answer. And if both parties have answering machines, it can easily take three or four back-and-forths before there is finally a live person at both ends of the wire. We're all guilty of carrying out entire conversations via voice mail or text messaging, when a simple phone call would have done the trick. The phone bill is the cheapest part of phone ownership and use. The time and concentration lost to unnecessary calls is worse than someone coming and dumping a barrelful of trash in your office every day.

You need to make some kind of move here to regain control of your "air space":

1. Stay aware of the length and content of all business calls. And make a little list of the points you want to cover before *you* call someone.

2. If you can't talk, don't answer. Especially true for cell phones (I hate 'em!). Don't bring them on luncheons or dates, don't talk loudly in public places about the most intimate aspects of your business, or, for that matter, your personal life. If you can't talk privately on your cell phone, don't answer!

3. Cultivate the fine art of cutting off time-wasters. Don't be ashamed to say things like "I don't believe I'm interested, but I appreciate your call" or "Thanks for calling, but I have a line of people/projects waiting for me right now. . . . "

> The more I avoid voice mail, answering machines, and cell phones, the more I get done. And the less cluttered my office schedule is. I don't work around a phone when I'm concentrating.

Security Sickness

Some offices have so much expensive stuff in them that protecting it becomes a preoccupation more compelling and time-consuming than the occupation we're supposedly there for. There's so much elegant stuff around that no one dares touch anything or even take a deep breath. And there's so much emphasis on guards, keys, safes, pass cards, codes, alarms, sentries, and security procedures that anyone visiting the office can clearly see that "it" is more important than they are. It's bad enough that we do this at home with our families (worry about and guard our treasures more than our kids); to do it at work is bad business. This all-out effort to police and protect is true mental clutter to us, and surely a downer to those who happen to share time or space with us in the office.

If you don't really want or need something enough to be worth all this, get rid of it!

Preoccupation with the Personal

Certainly our home and personal life goes on while we're at work, but letting the personal intrude too far into your job (especially if you work for someone else) is bad news. No matter how much they like us, no employer wants to have a project or program derailed or seriously delayed by a personal problem. Of course the personal is ultimately more important to most of us than business, but there is a time and place for it. Keeping it under control at the office is as important as organizing those highly visible papers on your desk.

Chapter 8
Ducking the Deluge: Preventing Future Clutter

The best way to save yourself from drowning is to get out of the water, and likewise, the plumber's first move, as your basement is filling and flooding with water, is to turn off the main. He cuts off the source, removes the cause, before he fixes the leak. When it comes to office clutter, we're usually too busy treading water to pull ourselves up and out or get ahead, and we never shut off the main valve.

How did things get this bad? Where did all this stuff come from?

We've got to identify the source and stop the inflow. Otherwise our office, no matter how clean we manage to make it, will rapidly be recluttered.

Ninety percent of office clutter can be traced to one or more of the following culprits.

Bureaucracy

Call it the company's fault if you will—this one is less under our control than other such types of office clutter. Certain tools, furnishings, manuals, notes, and records (for rear end covering) may be dictated as standard procedure. Even if you could do something faster and better with half the equipment and supplies (or entirely without them), there may be little or no choice about it. You don't need it but you must keep and carry it. This is a tough situation, and the only way out is to prove, politely, that your way is best.

Executive Envy

Many executives today are suffering from envy, and it can be deadlier than high interest rates. It manifests itself by constant straining to be an executive, an elusive position everyone admires and wants, though few even know what it is (and few would want it if they did!).

Executive is one of those power words we automatically assume is a plus and automatically respect if it's used with or added to anything. A downtown restaurant has good food at a good price, but sales are saggy until the owner discovers the power of the word *executive*. He raises the price, relabels the lunch special "the Executive Lunch," and sales triple!

Likewise, the word *executive*, when added to phones, pens, ties, airfares, autos, and hotel rooms, wins over all those witless souls who somehow believe it will raise them to executive-hood. Even if they can't actually have the position and the power, they can have a pile of executive stuff (always overpriced and underused) in their office.

Don't be suckered in by this!

Crutches and Pacifiers

The need for these is a common human weakness. When we lack, fail, stumble, grope, or struggle, our first impulse is to find a piece of equipment to fix things or "get us back on track." We've practiced and perfected this in everyday life, so when things heat up at the office, when the books are behind or out of balance, for example, or we've procrastinated ourselves into a hole, it's time to buy something to keep books better and faster. A bigger desk, another program, a "Cure Me" seminar—surely something will help me handle this situation. Yes, if I had a $400 letter opener that could open letters faster I'd have more time to answer them. A more advanced cabinet would streamline my filing. So instead of overcoming a weakness or coming to terms with a habit, we get a gadget.

> "We've moved from cardboard boxes filled with outdated litter, to neat wire baskets filled with outdated litter!"

Gifts

The number of business gifts or just plain old gifts that somehow end up in the office could almost rival paper as office pollution. When I ask people where they got the things around their office that they'd really like to dump, it's amazing how many say they were gifts! We get them and feel obligated to display them, or we use them and it's like grafting on a third thumb. The worst thing about gifts isn't just the necessity to show some appreciation for them, even if we hate them, but the obligation we feel to keep them.

Actually gift divestment should be a little easier in the office, because most of the gifts here aren't from charming three-year-olds or the love of our life—but merely from people who are trying to solicit our business. And many of those gauche gifts are from people who never set foot in our workplace (and if they did come into the office, you could always say the boss wouldn't let you hang it, or that you took it home, where all your really prized possessions are).

Gifts are one of those clutter switches that really need to be shut off. To help cut down gift clutter, give—and encourage others to give—only consumable gifts like fruit, candy, and cookies. Things like this can be set out somewhere in the office and they'll be gone without a trace by 3:00 P.M. Or do a good deed or favor for someone instead of giving a thing—it'll be remembered longer, and it's kindness without clutter.

A Big One—Vanity

Offices aren't just to work in; you may have noticed that for many they are also a way of gaining power and prestige for themselves while undermining others. Consulting for decades now with some of the world's largest companies, from Madison Avenue to Atlanta and Chicago and LA, I've witnessed full-grown, college-educated men and women pull maneuvers in this area that a third grader would be ashamed to own up to—such as a man refusing to go to someone else's office for a meeting because it put him in less of a "power" position than having people come to his office to meet. Or having a $70,000 remodeling job done to perfectly good offices so that one upper-level executive's office could be made a foot larger than all her colleagues' offices. Or having a heated argument over a quarter-inch difference in the nap of the carpeting in

one office versus another. In one huge company I worked with, the Engineering Department built the floor in their area of the building one foot higher, to assert their superiority over Sales.

Offices and their furnishings are too often seen as a way to gain an edge over others. Office space becomes a scepter or a whipping stick, and people count windows instead of customers. The game sometimes seems to be "Who Can Spend the Most?" I've cleaned rarely used $120,000 tables and $10,000 couches in offices, $600 ashtrays in offices where you can't even smoke. It's all vanity! This vanity doesn't stop at Wall Street or Peachtree Street or Hollywood or Scottsdale; it goes right down to the offices in schools, hospitals, stores, and even homes across the country—anywhere people use an office to uprate themselves.

The ultimate in offices as a badge of authority is a super-deluxe office—we cleaners call these "Mahogany Row." They include, of course, an executive bathroom, where I have had to handle complaints about the color of the toilet paper!

Idle Buying

The manufacturers, suppliers, and sellers of office supplies are among the best around at walking in with a catalog and notepad and walking out with a signed order for some gadget guaranteed to do double the work in half the time. In just one hour of listening to an office supplier's pitches, I came up with scores of seductive words and phrases to help saturate my office with more new toys. Any of the following sound familiar?

Workstation Slang That Seduces Us

- Designer
- Pressure sensitive (sexy, huh?)
- Invisible
- Removable
- Wood grain
- Self-seal
- Carousel
- Compact
- Modular
- Imprinted
- Embossed
- Monogrammed
- Reinforced
- Ultrasonic
- Ergonomic
- Biodegradable
- Solar-powered
- Stylish
- Distinctive
- Classic
- Elegant
- Executive
- Famous maker
- Full range
- Futuristic
- Top-of-the-line
- Finest
- Exclusive to us
- The original
- Commemorative
- Authentic down to . . .
- Unique

- Timeless
- Supple
- Limited edition
- Custom-made
- Cordless
- Wireless
- Portable
- Compatible
- Complete
- Mini
- Space-saving
- Genuine
- European
- Leather
- Leatherlike
- A set
- At last . . .
- Injection molded
- Antique
- Reproduction
- Handmade, -cast, -rubbed, -oiled, -painted, -decorated
- One of a kind
- No two alike
- At the touch of a button
- Just plug it in
- Preprogrammed
- Lighted
- Two (three, four, etc.) in one
- Travel size
- Sleek
- Slim
- Contemporary
- Digital
- Built-in sensor
- High-tech
- State of the art
- Advanced technology
- Patent applied for
- Free bonus gift
- Reorder online

And of course, the big clincher:

- **Free shipping!**

Anything with any of these characteristics has got to add character to our workspace, and at least double our image and output. Wrong! If something is solid gold and we don't need it, it is clutter!

When it comes to tools and equipment, for example, we're more likely to have too many than not enough. I was filmed for a *PM Magazine* TV segment once, and the shooting was done at the home of a local author of romance fiction.

When the TV people took a time-out to adjust the lighting, I asked her about her writing and she led me into an office you wouldn't believe. This was in the early days of computerdom—there was wall-to-wall computer equipment, including things I'd never seen (and I ran a multimillion-dollar payroll on computer twice a month). She had processors, printers, copiers, adjusters, mousers, transmitters, font selectors, spell checkers, hardware, software, and every-ware. Then breathlessly, she added, "I can move paragraphs."

I was taken aback by this array of technology—there wasn't a gadget she didn't have, an inch of uncovered space in this huge room. It had a highly official look and about as many reams of paper as in the entire American Express headquarters (which my company cleaned). I asked if she needed all this just to write novels. "Oh yes, these days there's no way you can write without good processing equipment." She was convinced that manual writing techniques were wiped from the earth with the birth of the computer and its endless accessories. We went back and they shot another scene or two, and at the next pause for camera repositioning I asked her how much she wrote. "A book every other year or so," she said. How many had they sold? "About 30,000 copies altogether," she said with a smile. As I headed off again to clean a window for the cameras, she ambled after me and said, "I hear you write."

"That's right."

"How many books have you done?"

"About two dozen in the last ten years."

"How many have they sold?"

"More than a million copies."

She paled as she went on to inquire, "What type of programs do you use?"

"I don't have a computer; I've never even touched one."

"So what do you use?"

"A 1959 Olympic manual typewriter."

At that point, she couldn't believe it. "Well, how do you move paragraphs?"

"I don't worry about that. With a manual I can write paragraphs that move the reader."

A few months later I noticed that when James Michener was asked by *Writer's Digest* how he put out all those big best-selling manuscripts, he smiled and said, "With an old Olympic manual typewriter."

Some of the biggest business deals, the most mind-boggling math solutions, the best poetry, music, and book manuscripts have been produced not only without a computer but without a typewriter of any kind, or even a desk. Just a pencil and a notepad.

Likewise, I can still beat my accountant in on-the-spot computations when it comes to figuring interest or square footage. He uses a calculator, and I do it with a ballpoint pen.

For a few years I almost lost my office ownership nerve, and the salespeople had almost convinced me that I was a dying breed because I didn't buy every new office automating machine that hit the market. I often got twice as much done each day as the people who did have all the latest gadgetry. But whenever something new was demonstrated, like those vegetable cutters on TV, it looked like a miracle, and I thought maybe I shouldn't miss out. Finally the office outfitting oracles convinced me that a nationally known writer and producer of many letters a day could not exist without a hand-held recorder that you could carry with you and use anywhere, even in the car. Just put your thoughts and messages on there and drop the tape on your assistant, who could then knock out all your letters. Sounded like a 50 percent improvement.

I struggled with that thing for six months, and the longer I used it the worse my letters got and the fewer went out. It took more of both my and my assistant's time to get a letter out. When something did get typed up, I had to read it carefully and revise it (most of us don't speak as well as we write, and some transcriptions would get garbled or be missing part of the thoughts or information). Then the letter or memo would have to be retyped, and I'd have to proof it and make sure the revisions were made correctly. All of this took longer than simply writing it out in longhand and then having it typed. And I lived in fear that something would be lost, erased, or missing from a building bid.

I thought perhaps the fact that I'd bought an inexpensive model might be the reason for my failure, so I went out and got a $1,500 one. It didn't help a bit. Writing things down would still have been 80 percent easier than rambling on about them. So I retired the new "helper" and got back up to speed.

After that I started asking some supermen and superwomen of the business world if they used Dictaphones, and the usual answer was, "You know, Don, I tried to use that thing for a year, and though others seem to make good use of them, I just couldn't."

It's amazing how much time and money we can waste trying to imitate "executives" (who are probably frustrated to tears with their latest gadget). I used to depend on office supply catalogs and salespeople (and professors in business classes) to learn what I needed to outfit my desk. Not anymore! I go to the real movers and shakers and find out what they use and don't use and why. The seasoned business pros have learned how to employ an office and desk efficiently under fire in the daily battles of business.

Just because it's there, new, modern, costly, and everyone else has one doesn't mean it's going to help you with your office overload. More likely it will add to it!

"Free" and Other Miscellaneous Clutter Sources

Suppliers, would-be suppliers, and clients are among the big sources here. We buy ten pounds of good, useful office materials, for example, and they throw in some worthless extra they couldn't sell and don't want and we'd never buy on a bet (but it's free, so we take it and we keep it). How many freebie key chains, baseball caps, calendars, tote bags, memo pads, and stick-on magnets do you have in your office right now? Even if these things aren't so poorly made that they self-destruct in the first six months of crammed drawer storage, we generally don't want to use something with someone else's logo on it in four-inch letters. So they kick around the office for years. Most free gifts are just bait for future clutter anyway: memberships, subscriptions, and more junk mail we don't want. You don't have to take the free snacks on the plane or anything that's free!

Freebie paper is an even bigger problem. At all the home shows, conferences, and conventions where I speak and do personal appearances, I see crowds filing past rows and rows of booths full of free printed material and salespeople on every side offering more. And everyone takes it because it's laid out or handed out and FREE. So they all come home with huge bags full of brochures and leaflets and catalogs and spec sheets and article reprints and advertisements and statistics. It is too much to get through anytime soon, so it is laid neatly in a pile next to the stuff collected at the last convention.

We'll even take stuff we *know* we'll never look at, if it's free. The key is to cut off all this right at the point of acceptance—don't take paper or flyers or "sample copies" that you don't really want or need just because they're free or offered or it's expected. That's what makes paper *work*.

The solution, the number one solution to the paper problem, is to cut down our intake of it.

Interior Decorators

Gads, the people who "decorate" our offices come up with some ugly stuff and leave us with it. Since they like it so well, send it right back to them as a gift. (What better revenge?)

Past Occupants

If a predecessor left it there, it may be one of the reasons they're gone! Unless you love it or it serves a real purpose, get rid of it fast!

Home Rejects

It's been pushed out of your home, under threat of death or divorce, and it somehow avoided the trash and ended up in the office.

Donations

Every time you donate something to charity, they give you a certificate or plaque (junk) to hang or keep somewhere (and probably use at least half of the donation money to buy and engrave it). Tell them you'll give if they don't!

Junk Mail

What's the big scapegoat for office clutter, what bears the most blame for our office overload, whose fault is it? Very few of us blame it on ourselves; we're all victims of that infamous junk mail. A man from Minnesota summed it up well: "My name is on the list of every political party and charitable organization in America. I am inundated with junk mail."

You folks who think your home office gets more than its share of junk mail haven't seen the half of it. The workplace is the real target. The junk mail at the office is bigger, thicker, on better paper stock, embossed, and the "Free Trial" bribes are even bigger and better.

Junk mail is a real contributor to the problem, but it isn't the cause. Junk mail doesn't arrive for no reason; *we* are usually the reason. We ourselves trigger much of our junk mail. Junk mail is expensive, often $1 a piece, to get into our hands. If there are 1 million of us getting that piece, some company is spending almost $1 million just to interest us. They don't and won't spend that stupidly. We asked them for something once, bought something from them or one of their partners, or at least tried it (to get the free gift).

Remember, when it comes to mail, that contact of any kind only generates further contact. One year when I was still in college, for example, the income pickings were meager and with our large and still young family, my wife and I just couldn't see our way to getting out Christmas cards that year. Barbara fretted about it and I betted about it. Most people send cards just because someone else sent *them* a card; we often do it more out of a sense of obligation than any real seasonal sentiment or desire to be in touch. So we just didn't send any cards out that year, and sure enough, we got about half the cards we usually did the next year. So we have just about quit sending cards—we did send gifts and photos to close friends and family, but we didn't follow address lists. Our incoming cards really dried up.

Feeling guilty about maybe being seen as the scrooges of the season, we began sending cards again. The more we sent, the more we received!

In business this phenomenon is even more pervasive. Contact with people for no real purpose ends up wasting a lot of time as well as paper. Some of us have no rhyme or reason to send someone something, but we toss a card or note in the mail anyway, or keep them on the mailing list, "just in case." Be more cautious. When people really need or want you or your services, in this day of online phone books and nationwide information services, they can find you in thirty seconds and not create any paperwork doing it.

Junk mail isn't the cause, you are. You or whoever previously occupied your position gave them some reason to seek you out. Taking the time today to cut off the stream will give you a lot of free time in the future.

> "In my company we had a guy who spent three hours every morning opening his mail (he received more mail than the rest of the corporate staff combined), reading through each and every magazine and piece of junk mail, then filling in cards and requests for more information (thus assuring that he would receive even more mail). We finally had to let him go—I think he went to work for the government."

My junk mail dwindles daily as I write "no" on the back of those return cards. I'm sure the solicitors appreciate it, too, not having to send a glossy full-color package to someone who's just going to chuck it unopened. What a waste of time, energy, and resources that is! Quit responding positively or even tentatively—when you join something (such as a book club) and then quit, they'll rag you forever. And there will always be a box somewhere on mail-order literature asking if they can spread your name around to others; be sure to notice it and say "no" to it.

You can write to a specific offending company and ask to be taken off their list. If you use the preaddressed business reply envelope, they'll even pay the postage. If you want to reduce the amount of unsolicited national advertising mail you receive at home, you may register with MPS by mailing your full name, address, city, state, zip, and phone number to: Mail Preference Service, Attn: Dept 13958038, Direct Marketing Association, PO Box 282, Carmel, NY 10512. Or register online at *www.dmaconsumers.org*.

Did You Direct Them to You?

Have you ever met people who complain about the food at a restaurant, yet continue to eat there? That's exactly like those who complain about all the mail they get because their name is in a professional directory. They hate all the mail, but they wouldn't want to be left out, so they keep okaying those yearly entry update forms. It's strictly up to you, remember. You're the one who'll have to handle the paper flow. You don't have to turn on the faucet just because it's in your house or you own one. On the other hand, you don't have to let it get the best of you. I receive five pieces of mail a day that I didn't ask for because my name is in professional directories. It gets the two-second recycle decision, so it never becomes a clutter problem.

E-mail

As we all know, there is a source of incoming clutter that won't make a dent in the landfill, but still weighs heavy on us. It's e-mail. Junk e-mail and spam are nuisances that rob our time. We have to sort through it looking for real correspondence, and they can even destroy our computers by spreading viruses. Too often when we need to find an important message, it is swimming amongst the come-ons for mortgage refinancing and prescriptions by mail.

Junk E-mail

If you're noticing that your inbox has more junk e-mails from strangers than from work associates, you need to do something about it. Be sure that you have a junk e-mail or spam filter in place. You can configure it to eliminate e-mails containing certain words or even sort e-mails from certain addresses into specific folders.

Whenever junk does get through the filter, see if you can unsubscribe to the mailing list. Most places require by law that companies offer an "opt out" on any e-newsletters they send. And, don't *ever* open up attachments in junk e-mails, or you could find you've spread a virus to every computer in your building. You can avoid electronic junk mail by not filling in forms soliciting information, and especially by withholding your e-mail address since it may be shared with other companies.

Magazines

Most of us in the office are faced with a flood of magazines, newsletters, newspapers, and monthly rundowns that started with one or two and then run up to twenty or thirty. Often, like the gush of a broken pipe, they arrive in groups of four or five in one morning's mail.

Some of this we're actually paying for: Review all your subscriptions and cut them back to the things you actually want or have time to read. You'll save guilt as well as time and money. (And don't add yourself to the routing slips of things you're not really interested in just to look good or "aware.")

Even for the complimentary issues we receive, every so often a little renewal form comes. Most of us just chuck it, and keep hoping that they'll stop coming because we've stopped reading. *They won't*, so check that "No thanks" box now and drop that baby in the mailbox—it usually doesn't even need a stamp.

Many companies and organizations have learned how to cleverly package additional sales or promotional literature as "newsletters" or "updates." Just because it's seasoned with a little hard information here and there doesn't mean you have to read it.

It helps with magazines to set a twenty-four-hour moratorium. Never let one lag into the next day. Then you'll get the value without the mess. Commit yourself to a quick turnaround, an instant decision, to act right now, the minute you get it. It's the only way to conquer it.

Remember, about 70 percent of most magazines are just advertising, which you can be sure will be repeated and updated in future issues. Only about 10 percent of the average magazine is of real interest to us. So scan the table of contents and clip the articles you really care about and carry them in your briefcase or planner. Read them while you're waiting for the car to be serviced or for the dentist to see you. Highlight anything you want to file or route and trash the article now if nothing is highlighted.

P.S. Bosses or company owners may not come out and say so, but they hate to see you flipping the pages of any kind of periodical or catalog on their time. Reports on what has already happened and predictions of what might happen too often crowd out what ought to be happening right now! Cutting down both the junk print and the time you spend on it could keep you from being cut out of raises and promotions.

Chapter 9
Clean Desk Secrets

No matter how many piles occupy our desktop, or how long it's been since we've seen the bottom of the inbox, we all secretly admire the "clean desk" operators. How do they do it? How can we do it—banish mess and confusion, and gain all that lovely, liberating, open workspace? It's not such a big secret, and not really hard . . . read on.

The Power of Paper

One of our staff came bursting into my office looking for a Band-Aid one day—he was bleeding badly.

"Wow! How did you do that?" I asked.

"On a piece of paper."

"You're kidding."

He wasn't. We've all had little slices and occasional bad cuts, right at our desk or table, from a soft, light, innocent piece of paper. Not only can paper deal us a flesh wound, it's a medium that carries good news, bad news, doom, salvation, information, inspiration, problems, and solutions. Think of it. Paper is the way we communicate about and record many aspects of life. Those little sheets of paper, so easy to rip, crumple, burn, or destroy, can delight or depress us, make us breathe faster or keep us awake, enrich us or bankrupt us. Can you believe that we big, strong, smart humans have let paper put us on the run? It puts a dread in all our lives. Tax time, for example, is paperwork, often a few-hour job, but by fighting it we manage to stretch it out to a two-week stress session.

Paper's cutting ability is nothing compared to its burying capacity. No matter how much we get through, more and more and more comes—loose, bound, letter size, legal size, colored, embossed, matte, gloss, and textured, it never stops. The paper overload has sneaked up on us gradually but from all directions.

My home insurance policy came the other day, for the same house and yard I've lived in for thirty years. A few years ago it was five pages; this time it was sixty pages of legal whereas and wherefores, with ten additional riders, in a large manila envelope. Likewise, the town I live in is no bigger now, but the size of the phone book has tripled. The phone bill, too, was once one page. Now if you count up all the pages in just one month's plain ordinary old home phone bill you will probably discover more than twenty pages of lists, separate little sub-bills and accountings, advisements and advertisements, explanations, thank-yous, and offers.

Paper is like the ever-thicker white blanket of a blizzard. There's no way you're going to stop the snow; you can only find a better way of shoveling and piling it to keep the path open. (Or of making sure that it slides right off your roof!)

Accumulation

There's nothing wrong with having a lot of stuff around. We often have to assemble a lot and spread it out and stack it up and sort through it to get anything done in life. The problem isn't creating a mess or even some chaos. That comes with accomplishment. The problem is leaving it all when you're done, or saving it to deal with later—constantly keeping or carrying stuff over until later: tomorrow, next week, next month, next winter, or sometime "when I get time . . ."

That which accumulates eventually clogs up and chokes out. There's only one answer, and that is to eliminate.

Leftover things that you didn't deal with, that you saved, even filed or stashed neatly, are still there. The best office system in the world, the best computer program, and even the best mind handling it all will eventually reach the point of fuse blowing. Or you'll spend all your time thrashing and hunting and digging and buying more programs and hiring more people to handle the accumulation and the aftereffects of the accumulation.

Look around you—very few great successful doers and producers let things accumulate. There's no set rule or way or time or anything else to handle accumulation, only one secret. . . . Don't allow it! It was bad enough a few years back. But today with all the quick means of communication around, e-mails and voice mails, and the reams of paper passing through our workplaces daily, you can have disaster in days.

> What's the single biggest bugaboo of desk and office
> clutter, according to everyone? . . . getting behind!

Your desk and workspace can be great and effective management tools for you. But if your space is so crowded with leftovers and accumulation you can't find it and use it, it will poison and pollute the fresh new business coming in and you'll find yourself just going in circles, working hard, feeling stressed, and getting nowhere. One of the best management principles in the world is to take care of something right after you finish working with it—clean it up, repair it if necessary, and put it away. Don't wait until the next morning or right before you need it next to get it ready.

When I was a boy, the farmers who prospered were the ones who woke up in the morning with everything ready to go. Their barns, milk buckets, and cream separators were clean and they were able to go to work instantly. The others, who left leftovers around and the little things for later, took twice as long to get something done, and the sun was up and half the day wasted before they hit the fields.

I grew up loving the idea of readiness. If all was cleaned up and taken care of before you went to sleep, you felt good and slept well and were able to start a new day on new stuff. If the first thing you face in the morning is something long overdue or half done, you're not just off on the wrong foot, but less than eager to get going.

With my many businesses and big family as well as community and other outside activities, the idea of allowing no accumulation in my office was one of the most liberating things I've ever learned. Make this a policy at your desk, and even if you're usually inundated with thirty more projects than most people would want to take on, you will always come to work with no leftovers.

When I hit the desk in the morning, if I discover I have to leave right then to go to Brisbane or Phoenix, or have a sudden rush assignment from *USA Today*, I can do it right that minute because I have no backlog or reservoir of undone stuff to do. When I walk in, I can jump right on any mail that's there or any calls that come in. I can do them right then, not place them in a line behind other "overdues." If you pile them, they, too, instantly become leftovers—accumulation.

Most people have scores of long-range projects underway or on the drawing board that may take years to finish, but I'm talking here about the daily "to dos" and the regular everyday, weekly, monthly workflow: answering calls and letters, reading e-mails, preparing proposals and reports, meeting deadlines, and so on. Never leave any work on your desk at the end of the day; when you leave, it should be clear—every big and little thing that was scheduled to be done that day should be done. Leaving anything very long in your office makes it and you feel at home. Once you accept the idea of it piled there, you are dead in the clutter water! Deal with it as soon as it appears, and one of the best ways to do that is to carry it with you (see page 147).

"But I Can't Do It Now!"

Many people tell me this can't be done, and they ask me, where do I get the time? I'll let you answer your own question. You end up doing it all in the end anyway, even if you're working three weeks or three months behind. And doing it the "later" and "too late" way takes much more time (just as dishes left to sit take longer and are a lot harder to do because the plates are all stuck together and the egg and syrup have hardened on them). So don't ask, "How in the world do I manage to have no leftover or accumulated stuff?" You'll have the time to do things right away once you don't have to do all that extra work—that "double time" or more everything takes to do when you've let it wait awhile. And you won't have to do all that suffering in between!

You can put things off, but you can't be rid of them till they're done, so why not do them right now while you have them in hand? Exactly *how* you deal with each piece of paper is up to you. Just start today, and don't let anything accumulate. Get it all done and then arrive to work each day with all of yesterday's daily and little detail work done. Then watch your efficiency and people's respect for you rise, and watch out, you may even get a raise.

This is the whole purpose of all the "daily planners"—not forgetting things and doing them on time. Even if you do have time later to do something, move it up to now and do it now. Always arrive at the meeting and on the job or the playing field ready to play. You'll play much better. This is *the* key to office control and dynamite management.

Paper Processing in Brief

Hundreds of books and articles have been written on the "paper war," detailing all kinds of ingenious tactics and techniques to handle it. Not a few of these programs to reduce the paper proliferation (like more elaborate filing systems, computerizing everything, etc.) actually create and cause more paper problems in the end. So let me save you the trouble of reading all that and just give you the bottom line of victory over paper:

1. Don't ever think that any magic tool or person is going to just lift the whole burden from you.
2. Deal with each piece right away, while it's still fresh in your mind, right when you first look at it. Or if you can't do that right now, carry it around with you and think about it in your less valuable driving, waiting, and dozing time, until you've figured out what you're going to do: define the problem, come up with a solution, or figure out what you have to do before you can deal with it. Then *do* it!

The following table may speed your paper-pitching efforts—the higher the number, the higher the junk quotient.

Junk Likelihood by Location in the Office	
Likelihood	**Location**
20	In boxes in backroom
19	In boxes on office floor any old place
18	In boxes under desk
17	In or on credenza
16	On top of file cabinet
15	In any old drawer
14	On spindle
13	In bookcase
12	On bookcase
11	In files
10	"To be filed" pile
9	"To be filed" overflow
8	In paper organizer
7	In miscellaneous stacking trays on desk ("in limbo" boxes)
6	Inbox
5	Outbox
4	In desk drawer
3	In briefcase
2	On desktop (the farther away from the desk jockey, the less valuable)
1	In safe

The Ins and Outs of Inboxes

Like me, you've probably tried about every type of desk tray in an effort to regulate your daily paper flow and have discovered that few if any are perfect. The reason is simple, as I teach the kids at my "Getting Acquainted with Cleaning" grade school assemblies. I tell them I'll give them a big prize if they can identify the most important, even magical, tool for taking care of their room. Then I hold up a clothes hanger and yell out, "What is this?"

An immediate chorus comes back, "A hanger!"

"Right," I say. Then I ask, "What does it do?"

Now 500 enthusiastic kids yell back, "Hangs up clothes!"

"It does?" I question. "*Okay*, let's be quiet and watch." Then I hold up the hanger, and stare at it . . . for a minute or two, and all is quiet in the entire auditorium. By now the kids are getting a little confused and are murmuring. Finally, I yell out, "It isn't working. You told me it hangs up clothes and it isn't doing anything."

Then a wave of wisdom ripples through the group, and finally a little voice pipes up and says, "Well, ah, Mr. Aslett, you have to put the clothes on it. . . . "

"Ah ha," I say, "It holds the clothes, doesn't it. Who hangs up the clothes?"

By now they're getting the message loud and clear, and they yell back, "*We* do!"

Those little in, out, over, under, high, low, plastic, wood, metal, or whatever trays in your office are identical to the hanger. They hold papers and that is all. Even the labels on them don't mean a thing without you. Too often when we get another assignment, add another person or job that we're responsible for, we add a tray and figure that takes care of it.

In fact, it just means yet more accumulation. The more places to stash and stack, the more things in limbo.

These things are tools, not workers. Unless you have them programmed into a system that really works for you, they just sit there and feast on indecision. They can be a liability, actually impeding the flow, like a miniature dam.

We do need to subdivide the flow—those "In" and "Out" designations are really for other people's convenience—so they'll know where to put fresh stuff and when to take away the old. *We* have to take the incoming and sort it into action categories. My own categories, for example, are File, Send For, Cut Up, Route (to Someone Else), Respond Today, Respond Soon, and Do It!

To keep any of our trays or boxes from becoming backwaters, the whole secret is making sure each has been *emptied* by the deadline we set for it—daily, weekly, or whatever.

Set a Time and Place for Paper Paring

The fresh inflow of paper each day and week is such that you do have to keep after it, or it'll start piling up again. Yes, you do have all kinds of rush projects and other priorities, but you must allow some time for this essential activity, a place in your schedule for paper paring down and filing and other important measures of clutter reduction. It's the key to keeping that priceless feeling of being in control.

Try the first fifteen minutes of each new day, for example. We usually feel nice and aggressive then, plus we are eager to get to and through the daily quota of decluttering so we can get on to the more exciting things on the agenda.

You could also do it weekly, the first hour of every Friday, for example. Just make sure that it's done often and faithfully and not too long at a stretch. All decluttering, and especially paper decluttering, takes emotional energy as well as physical, and if you try to do too much at once you'll fizzle out.

Finished Project Clutter

A category of paper accumulation we office folk are especially guilty of is finished project clutter. There's always so much going on, so many new and urgent directives and agendas, that the dismantling and disposing of the old and finished always seem to get lost in the shuffle. If we dodge this duty long enough, however, there will eventually be nowhere to even set down a new project, and anything we do still need from the old will be unfindable.

Some finished project management thoughts from a fellow writer:

"When I finish a book or manual, I give the project a couple of weeks for the dust to settle, then I clean the shelves, the file cabinets, and computer of everything specifically related to that project. I sort the notes (trashing everything that was incorporated into the book or otherwise dealt with) and dump the remainder into a box with the page proofs, correspondence files, artwork, and a complete disk backup of the computer files. The box is then labeled with the name of the book or manual, and stashed well out of my working space until I do revisions or it looks like a good time to throw the whole thing out."

Opening Mail

Most of us start to open it, shuffle it around, and then set it all down somewhere in a heap. The right way to do it is standing right over a trash can.

Dump the junk mail right in: the solicitations from the Cheese and Crackers Foundation, the promise of a sample pen with "Your Company Here" stamped on it, and those card decks an inch thick. They all just take up time and generate further junk mail!

Whenever possible, handle each piece of mail only once. For example, slit open a credit card bill, drop the torn envelope into the can and save the return envelope; then grab the corner of the invoice and shake. Out fall the circulars for turbo calculators, scented stuffers, promotional enclosures, and other bits you don't want, right into the trash. Slip the bill into the flap of the return envelope and put all the bills together in one stack.

Divide the rest of the incoming mail into two more piles: correspondence, and then a third pile of newsletters, magazines, etc. (anything that doesn't require a timely answer, that you *would* like to take the time to read). Shake the magazines over the can to get rid of any card inserts that will only become loose clutter later.

As for those catalogs, of everything from executive whatnots to computers, they call for a snap judgment: Add to the Peruse Later pile, or drop in the can. Whatever you do, don't start thumbing through them now; don't stop your day for something you didn't ask for or want.

YOU'RE DONE! You've disposed of the bulk, and the bills are all together so that they can be put wherever you keep your payables without fear of losing track of any. You can act on the correspondence now and look forward to flipping through the reading matter over lunch.

Keep It Together!

Another secret of the real doers is keeping stuff that belongs together actually together, not leaving anything loose or in a position to come apart. One of the biggest time wasters in any office is hunting down and putting back things that have gotten separated in the shuffle.

The first thing to do with papers that belong with each other or to a particular project is to bind, staple, or tape them into a single unit. Then, when a coworker goes through the pile, a sudden wind gust blows through the office, or you drop the whole thing in the hall, all the pieces stay together.

In the stretch, I've found rubber bands a real asset here. They're cheap and easy to use and they hold loose things in one neat unit better than clips or staples, even a *lot* of stuff.

What Should You Do with That "Unfinished Business"?

In life and production, there is a principle called flow, the smooth continuous running (of water, or projects in progress). We put something in one end and it comes out the other.

Yes, Even Paper Clips...

These things can generate more stress than paper does. Tests show that of all the millions of paper clips released into the office "stream," at best one in six actually achieves its original purpose of clipping paper. All the rest are used for ear cleaning, free-form sculpture, garlands, toys for kids, shooting rubber bands, filling crevices, fidget devices for nervous or unoccupied people, and testing the tolerance of the janitor's vacuum.

Once used or removed from a piece of paper, they usually become clutter, because like empty bullet cartridges, they seldom make it back to a storage place for reuse. In thirty-five years of office cleaning and office work, I have never figured out a clip cure. So I just converted to a little piece of clear tape in one corner for holding papers together. Less problem, less litter, less lost pages, and less snagging, too. Try it! It may stick with you, and it beats getting "clipped" any day.

• • • • • • • •

When we don't see much coming out the other end of the pipe, however, not nearly as much as went in, we know there is a restriction, a snag, a place where the flow is stopped or slowed. So we hunt and tap and poke and listen, then finally find and remove it and things gush through again.

In an office, one of the major restrictions in paper flow is material waiting for something—an answer, approval, confirmation, a signature, a check, a call, an address. You've gone as far as you can with them, but for various reasons some of the pieces of paper passing into your office can't leave, but must remain. There's always a risk of this held-up stuff mixing with the moving stuff and delaying it, too. This is a real problem with things on hold.

In my office we've learned to take things like this and tuck them immediately into a boldly labeled file folder, inside of a "special action" or "holding pattern" box in plain sight and reach (mine is right on top of my desk). Then, every morning after the mail comes in—or at least at the beginning and end of every week—we check the box for things whose missing piece has materialized so that they can be on their way.

Don't file it or you'll forget it—*out* is active!

How to Make Sure It Gets in the Mail

Another big backwater of offices (and homes, too) is stuff that didn't quite make it into the mail. Willing it into the mail won't do it—you have to actually get it into the hands of the U.S. Postal Service or UPS or whomever. So set up a system that makes it quick and easy to mail things. So often we have something in hand, we know exactly where to send it (and it's brilliant, kind, or just plain profitable to do so), but the difficulty of packaging it up, finding envelopes or boxes, and getting it to the post office or the pickup point puts us off. So we hang on to it and pile or set it somewhere, and the impulse is bogged down or lost. Or if we can't dump it on someone else (a generous coworker or an assistant) to perform these last mundane little preliminaries for us, it just sits there and doesn't go anywhere.

Every one of us should have a small mailing center in a handy drawer so that if we have something to mail to someone, in twenty seconds we can just fold or roll it up, stuff it in, stamp, and ship it!

A Big One: Briefcases

Many of the people I queried for the first edition of this book said that they didn't carry a briefcase. To me, having a briefcase is more important than having a bathroom—I can't imagine being without one. Then I thought back to when I was starting my business—I had a lot going on then, too, but I didn't have a briefcase. I did have stuff all over and around my desk. Now I have a big active briefcase and little or nothing hanging around my desk. Briefcases fit my style of paper handling, working on the go, and often working at home as well as the office.

In our busy world today many of us don't live at our desks. Even if we have a full-time office job, we may still be out and away from the building much of the time. And when we are there, unfortunately, the follow-up calls and the fresh calls and all those people who just "drop by" occupy most of our time. It's hard to settle in and get the real long-range stuff done at an office desk. When I realized this, I started loading up the day's work as well as long letters and the "let me think on this" things into a shallow cardboard box and carrying them with me in the car, while traveling, or when headed home. Having it all with me was a real advantage.

Then I made the move to a cheap briefcase, which soon broke down under the load. I went to a better one and loved the convenience. It saved me a lot of time and was the perfect relief valve for my desks. By carrying scissors, tape, a ruler, and some notepads, etc., I converted my briefcase into a portable office. By now I was using the biggest, best one I could find, and it served about a year and then it, too, was beat. Finally I bought a king-size aluminum unit for $350, and no desk has ever served me better.

Using a briefcase as an accessory office, I can get three times the work done. I can make good use of every waiting minute (and there are plenty of them in modern life, even if you don't spend as much time on the go as I do).

Much paperwork is actually time-fragment work. We don't get hours anymore to study and peruse things. We get minutes, here and there, and if you have the easy-to-process stuff with you when a free moment appears, you can knock it off right on the spot. You can work in the house when the kids are asleep, or at the doctor's office waiting for your appointment, or the airport while waiting for your flight.

If you keep a supply of "short note" stationery with you, you can handwrite brief friendly answers to letters, and inquiries that can be sent as is. Or write out instructions to your staff for taking care of things—outline the response you want right in the margins of the letter or memo. You can knock off many "to dos" by making a quick call to someone, with his or her letter in hand and the phone. You can also "de-bulk" the incoming stream. I always carry two or three fresh, empty files with me, put the gems that I mine from the mass in there, and bring them back to the office.

Briefcases can help with magazines and junk mail, too. Toss the magazines and junk mail packets that arrive in your case, not on your desk.

If you have those magazines with you, it's amazing how quickly, enjoyably, and unobtrusively you can plow through them and strip them down to the page or two you might want to save for your files. I'm never behind even a day or two on magazines, but I see plenty of people stack reading material in a "when I get time" pile, and after a little while they say to themselves, "Well, it's getting old now, so no rush," and they just pile more on top. The deeper the pile, the less likely we are to ever read anything in it.

I've never had much of an urge to snoop into other people's property, but briefcases intrigue me. Most of them have had so little use they look brand new, and whenever anyone snaps one open on the plane, train, or in a meeting, I sneak a glance in that direction. Often I'm amazed at the contents. Why do many people even carry them? Inside you see pens, a ticket, maybe a map, a magazine or a novel, a couple of business cards, a roll of breath mints or a few toothpicks, and a bottle of aspirin.

As you can tell by now, I take briefcases seriously. I find them a good solution for keeping current, helping to keep my desks uncluttered. If you've just been a casual briefcaser up to now, try packing one with all those overdue-to-be-tended-to desktop papers. It won't just keep them fresh and unwrinkled, it'll prevent further procrastination.

Drawers: A Neglected Secret of Office Organization

Drawers offer hidden space to save face, and even some built-in storage discipline—they won't close when they're too full!

Drawers are really wonderful things, yet so many of us use even our most important and convenient drawers to store junk—old, dead, inactive stuff. Much of what's out on our desk in piles, on the other hand, we actually use, but it's in the way. It could be in a drawer, just as accessible as on the desk. A drawer isn't a hiding place or idle storage; think of it as a closed desktop, serving the same purpose, only with protection and privacy.

This was a great discovery in deskology for me. So I converted my middle desk drawer into a second desktop—scooped up all those extra pens and message pads and desktop tools all over and put them all in there neatly. They were still at my fingertips, just about four inches lower—what a gain in clean, uncluttered workspace!

A couple of secrets to dynamic drawer use:

1. The most distant drawers should contain the least frequently used stuff.

2. Whenever possible, dedicate each drawer to one basic thing. Amazing how this helps with organization and speed of use. My desk, for example, has a Letter drawer, a To Do drawer, and a Tool drawer. You might want to have one for stationery and envelopes only, or writing tools only.

3. Mark the purpose on the outside. You might *know* what's in there, but a label is affirmation and commitment.

And at the Bottom . . .

That ever-present odds and ends clutter at the bottom of every drawer: golf tees, even in the desks of nongolfers; bank and car dealership key rings; pounds of coins (pennies, nickels, Canadian); parts—clasps, locks, hinges, handles, screws, unidentifiable plastic pieces—that broke or fell off something. Dead batteries, game pieces, single earrings, hair ties, bottle caps, lost buttons, nametags and lapel pins, banjo picks, swizzle sticks, single shoestrings, twist ties, ball bearings, lenses from old sunglasses, a picture of someone's baby (you don't remember whose), a couple of beat-up pills that you can't identify, etc., etc. Many of us dodge drawer cleaning so that we don't have to figure out what to do with this stuff! The only cure is to stop tossing odds and ends into drawers to get them out of sight.

• • • • • • • •

Wall Mounting Cuts Clutter

Too many things on the desks and tables? If there is any office paraphernalia that can be wall mounted, do it. Wall-mounting the phone in an office, for example, saves it and all its sidekicks from hogging that premium desktop space. It is a good idea to mount anything you can, to get it out of the way and away from your elbow swing. It saves a lot of cleaning and dusting, too. And this is even easier for cube-dwellers, with the vast array of slotters and stackers, shelvers and hangers available to accessorize cubicle walls. Here are a few office inhabitants that can be wall mounted:

- Telephones
- Message boxes
- Lighting
- Hooks or racks for hats, coats, and umbrellas
- Bookcases and shelves
- Miniature closets
- Fans
- Pencil sharpeners
- In- and outboxes
- File pockets and trays

- Catalog racks
- Calendars
- Clocks and thermometers
- Maps and plans
- Photographs and pictures
- Trophies
- Awards
- Plaques
- Displays
- Plants
- Speakers

Clutter-Free Computing

Today's giant hard drives are like having a garage that's forty miles long—you can store as much junk as you want, it seems. But too much on your hard drive (like too many clothes in a tightly packed closet) still means you have to sort and sift—and in the case of the computer, scroll—through all the stuff you rarely or never use, to reach what you do want. And it multiplies the chance of errors and confusion.

If you have an older machine, storing junk on it really reduces the computer power available for key tasks and programs. So here are a few secrets of keeping computers clutter-free:

1. "Save, save" may be the mantra of computerdom, but try to avoid mindless saving of everything (like the not-so-good jokes your brother-in-law keeps sending you). Some things should just be enjoyed quickly and then deleted.

2. Naming documents, disks, and CD-ROMs as descriptively as possible saves time when going back through to determine what's outdated, and for that matter when using your files every day. So be as clear as possible to avoid endless opening and closing of the wrong documents, and try to avoid titles like "Misc. Stuff."

3. Even if space is not an issue, run your eye over the contents of your hard drive periodically and move projects that are no longer current or active to Zip, CD, or other off-computer storage.

4. Videos and images take up LOTS of space, so only keep the ones you really like or still need (that means ditch the e-mail of twenty different sidewalk drawings after you've enjoyed it once or twice).

5. Extra copies and earlier drafts of documents and reports and the like can cause very time-costly confusion. So identify each stage of these clearly, and move out (to a Zip drive or whatever) the ones you don't need anymore as soon as you can. Or delete the extras when you're sure they are no longer needed.

6. If you have programs that came with the computer that you never use, and never intend to, or older versions of programs, consider uninstalling them.

7. Many computers and programs also have other things that came with them, which we may never need or use or

don't need to keep on the computer: the copy of Simple-Text/QuickTime that a new program included to be sure you had one, when you already have two copies of it from other programs on your drive; the tutorial for a program that you have already mastered; or copies of the program license agreement in a dozen languages, just in case. Move things you are sure you don't need (or don't need now) to off-computer storage as necessary.

Calendars

These can be a prime piece of paper clutter. Sure we need to know what day it is, but only when we need to know what day it is! Even when I was a kid, everyone had extra calendars—from the hardware store, the dairy, the bank, the feed mill, and every other business around. My folks and uncles wondered where to put them. Some of them were too valuable to throw out because of the little thermometers on them.

Then I grew up and the calendars only seemed to increase and multiply. There were company calendars, calendars from every supplier or would-be supplier, giant calendars and year-at-a-glance calendars and all kinds of miniature calendars, even calendars on wristwatches and computers. Plus all the beautifully illustrated ones people give you at Christmas. In an effort to use up more of them, I began to designate different calendars for different purposes, and ended up missing some events and appointments only because I'd been looking at the wrong calendar.

One day I finally realized the only fully useful calendar is one you carry with you. (I learned this by watching most people go to their wallet or checkbook when they needed to find a date.) Now I have and use only a single calendar—the one in my schedule book or planner. After all, your desk isn't the only place you need to know the date, and there isn't a wall handy all the time. And a blotter calendar has to be cleared off every time you want to make an appointment.

For scheduling and notes, bigger is better—a calendar with squares big enough to write in everything you need to (and *read* it afterward).

Try the calendar cure for a year (having only one and carrying it with you), and watch how much paper goes away! It saves space and trouble and the ownership of forty of them. In this day of newspapers, TV, radio, and computers, you'll rarely be at a loss for the date anyway.

Today's PDAs (personal digital assistants) have endless calendaring and note- and list-keeping capabilities with alarms and pop-ups to remind you of appointments or special occasions.

P.S. I remember a farmer in my area once who filed for divorce because his wife had ripped down his calendar, which (he noted in his court claim) had all the breeding dates and birthdays of the animals in his registered dairy herd, their health and butterfat test results, addresses of hay sources, etc. So don't just check those old calendars for nice pictures before you chuck them. Check for any notes or records.

Addresses

We all know why . . . but where and how do you keep addresses? They end up one of the biggest clutter-breeding entities in an office. Look right now at how many gadgets, systems, books, files, and cards you have or have had just to keep them. Addresses are important, too—we're always looking for one, and we're eager to save it and have it available when and if we need it. Addresses are, in fact, the jugular vein of clutter flow; they're largely responsible for how much paper goes in and out of an office or anywhere. Addresses are even profitable now, as you know if you've ever bought a mailing list.

Every office planner and get-yourself-organized course attempts to set up a foolproof way to store addresses, but I've never seen or heard the perfect way. I do have a couple of rules, though:

1. Keep addresses *with you,* always. They do little good if they're available only at the office. PDAs and other credit-card-sized storers of info like this are great as long as they work. Too often, when we really need them is when the battery goes dead or some other glitch develops.
2. Feed every new address that comes your way (on a business trip or in a phone or luncheon conversation) into your system right away. Whether it's a little black book or the most advanced digital address book, *immediately* enter any address changes you become aware of. Don't wait till your staff has sent three letters to the old address. *Keep that address file current!*

Bulletin Boards–Tool or Trial?

Bulletin boards are a real love/hate item in "officedom." They can all too easily be ugly or just a compounding of the clutter, but you can count me among the bulletin board lovers. A well-used bulletin board is not only a touch of personality and more attractive than a still life or landscape, but also a key "wall map" of information. It stops people and passes along facts and messages, without interrupting what you're doing.

I began my love affair with these cork-complexioned beauties while cleaning offices, where all too often I had to remove tape and patch pinholes where people had just "hung stuff" on nice walls. If it has to be hung—and there's much to be said for keeping things in sight—a bulletin board is the place to do it. It can be a "picture window" into humor and intrigue as well as instruction and inspiration.

On a bulletin board it's up and out of the way, so it won't get lost or have to be moved or cleaned around. This is a good paper reducer, too—you can post one sheet (picture, letter, announcement, copy) instead of passing them out all over.

Make a bulletin board work for you. You'll love it, and it will help organize your office. Mine gets more smiles and remarks than the best art I've ever had on the wall. If you don't want to go the whole route, just try a little bite-sized board.

The catch, of course, is keeping them up (as in "up to date"). People who use bulletin boards as a place to dispose of things that they then proceed to forget entirely give us b.b. freaks a bad name. On most bulletin boards at least 40 percent of what's so proudly displayed is long defunct. Bare bulletin boards are about as damaging, giving the message all too clearly that "nothing is going on around here."

Keeping them current is the whole secret. When you start putting one thing on top of another or shifting six things around to find a spot for something new, it's time to dejunk. When a new joke or display comes along and there's no space, some of the old ones must go. That's the law of the cork jungle. (Having a different person in the office assigned to check the board each month is a good way to keep it decluttered.)

One Last Clutter Saver—Pay Cash!

One of the little secrets of reducing desk (and administrative) clutter is to pay cash for expenses related to your company. Paying cash is quick and it cuts quite a few pieces of paper out of already overflowing files. You just have to be sure to get a receipt for anything you purchase. The other day, for example, our office was buying something for $50. I heard two of my staff spend at least fifteen minutes each getting together pages of credit information, etc. "Gadfrey," I interrupted. "We have money; just send them a check with the order!" That had never occurred to anyone. Filling out and copying all five pages of that credit application, mailing it in, and then handling the minimum four more stages the transaction would undoubtedly involve would end up costing more than the item itself. Carry a checkbook with you or use your debit card to pay cash on the spot. And watch how much wasted time and unnecessary bookkeeping disappears from your life.

Another good idea is to keep $20 to $50 cash in your desk or office. Then have a petty cash voucher there, so you can account for all of it, or just forget worrying about keeping precise track of every cent of this for income tax deductions. I guarantee the convenience is worth the 30 percent tax loss on such minor amounts (and I'm not sure that it is a loss, by the time you consider the value of your time spent in bookkeeping). It's the same principle as having a change tray in your car for toll roads and parking. The seasoned, efficient, smart people always have a little pool of cash there at hand. It saves fishing through pockets, getting up to find your purse or wallet, fiddling with checkbooks and credit cards, and piles of paper. Think how many tiny payments you have to make in a week, even just to lend someone lunch money. If you need a receipt or someone comes around with an office collection, it's right there. You don't need to make it a Wells Fargo stop, just a convenience store for cash. Trust me, it cuts office clutter!

A Few More "Clean Desk" Secrets

I've worked around some pretty impressive office users in my time, and I'd like to share their clutter-cutting tactics with you here.

One business wizard I know had sixteen profitable corporations at last count. Yet he has a superneat office with only one desk and zero assistants. Yep, you heard right—he gets as much done as ten average office workers, his stuff is neat and accurate and on time, and he has no assistants at all. Just a desk and a file and a notebook or two and some pens. Every time I visit his office or work around him, I say it can't be done, but he does it, and he's never in a hurry, either. He can produce any sales offer, proposal, or prospectus he needs to instantly. He's a builder, contractor, Realtor, lessee, and insurance broker; he owns and manages apartment buildings and has partners all over the place. Yet he's always thoroughly organized when you call or drop by. I stand in awe at each visit, so I finally asked him how he does it.

"The bottom line of my business and office operation is reduced detail. Lots of people like detail, like to create it and wallow in it, fight it and play at business in it. I don't like it. Ninety percent of detail comes from indecision and putting off action. People can't make up their minds, so they wait and wait and wait and lay things aside until they can. By then they're buried.

"When I open mail, immediately, I either throw it away or put it away. If it needs answering, I don't believe in too much formality, just get the job done now and right. So I write the answer right on the bottom of the letter and send it back. In fact, my idol (a fellow who runs twenty-two corporations) uses handwritten notes for everything—it's quick, cheap, and personal. And it sure beats 'delegation,' formality, and a lot of built-in chances for mistakes.

"I don't have excess anything in my files, so there's no place to lose anything. Lastly, I pick and do only the kinds of business and work that I really like. What you like, you'll take care of. I don't like inventory and lots of payables and receivables, so I keep my bookkeeping very simple and straightforward and keep that sort of thing to a minimum."

I also know a CPA whose ability to produce clean, sharp work and a tremendous amount of it really impresses me. No matter how busy he is, you will never go into his office and find a mess on his desk. Even if you arrive for an all-day conference or income tax session, there isn't even a germ in there. He doesn't just work for me full-time, he also keeps records and books for many other businesses, is district Scout commissioner, treasurer of the Lion's Club, holds several church positions, and heads a family of seven children.

Intrigued by how much he gets done without ever leaving any of the "evidence" around, I finally pinned him down early one morning and asked him his secret.

"I might have thirty projects going, but I only keep one in hand (and on the desk) and focus on it till it's done. No use in having twenty-nine others there right under my nose or elbows while I'm working on the one; they'd only distract me. So as soon as the one I'm working on is done, or as far as it can go, I put it away using my own system, as we all should, for keeping track of it until it becomes active again. As soon as I'm done with something, I get it out of sight and out of the way of the next project."

The Ten Commandments
of
Office Uncluttering

Thou shalt have no priority above keeping thy office neat and clutter-free always.

Thou shalt not cover usable space with clutter.

Thou shalt not pile or stack . . . on desks, tables, floors, file cabinets, or anywhere.

Thou shalt not keep more than three copies of anything.

Thou shalt not covet thy neighbor's copier, computer, fax machine, or bookcases.

Thou shalt not buy a new or bigger hard drive, credenza, or file cabinet rather than dejunk the old.

Thou shalt not kill correspondence, phone messages, or proposals by holding onto them indefinitely.

Thou shalt SORT all papers that come into thine hands immediately—and keep them sorted—for jumbled papers are the root of all evil and demoralization.

Thou shalt never let the To Be Filed pile rise higher than four inches.

Thou shalt not lay down anything from the files anywhere once thou art finished with it. Put it right back!

Thou shalt discard all old magazines regularly (at least quarterly), unless thou art a doctor's office.

Chapter 10
Overcoming Fear of Filing

When you finally narrow down to the things that really are worth keeping, it's like roundup day on the ranch. Now you have them there, off the range and in your office, and they're mooing and prancing and milling around (that's what unfiled stuff does, you know). You can't just let them sit there—before long they all have to go somewhere, be shipped out or moved to their new pasture, stored or refrigerated or canned.

This is the law of the harvest, whether it's cows, eggs, fresh-picked tomatoes—or papers. When you've finally found it or got it together, while you still remember what and where it all is, it has to be "put up." Or for sure it will be wasted or go bad and double your handling time, and make you look dumb or frustrate you when you need it again.

You have to put things where you can find them, and in the office this process is usually called *filing*.

If It's Not in the File, It Doesn't Do You Any Good

There are at least as many people afraid of filing as of flying. In the case of filing, they are afraid that in the process they might lose those important papers that are their lifeline. Well, both flying and filing are far less hazardous than piling up papers and having anything of value buried and suffocated as a result.

A lot of office clutter comes from failure to file. We're not sure how to do it or we hate to do it, so we dodge it. The secret is to personalize your filing system. If you set up your own system, you'll not only know how but you'll love to use it and it will work. If you try to follow some program you've never liked or understood, you'll fight it forever, and your desk and office will look and feel like a battleground.

The first few times people told me they carried their money in their socks, their matches in their hat, their keys in their bra, a toothbrush in their lunch bag, directions written on a napkin—I laughed. Now that I have a little more life experience, I know that what works for you is the most important ingredient in anything.

This is only more true of filing. There is no "one way" to do it. Any advice or instruction about filing should just give you ideas and options, not exact patterns. Your filing system needs to fit you and your personality, your goals and interests and what you are doing. No two people are the same when it comes to this, and you have all kinds of options. You can also make up your own ways or combinations of ways.

My office is the headquarters for several corporations. There's a great deal of stuff coming in and out at all times, and we have to keep precise records on most of it. When the phone rings and ABC Chemical or an insurance company calls and wants to know something, or we need an address we haven't used in six years, my people have it in seconds, and they all file differently than I do. Sometimes my editor's piles look chaotic to me, but she never loses anything and can retrieve something in seconds. She knows her stacks. My general manager and publicist, Tobi, has her own way of filing, too. She's shown me her filing categories in case I need to find something while she's out, and I can use her system, but I'd never handle things that way myself because it's confusing to my way of thinking. Our filing tools are different, too. I like to have everything in front of me in tangible form, in a notebook. She says this is old-fashioned and keeps hers in the computer so that she can just push a button to pull out a copy. Each is different, but it works.

The basic purpose of filing is very simple:

> To keep something and be able to find it fast, to keep something and be able to find it fast, to keep something and be able to find it fast. . . .

Just those two principles repeated over and over. All you need to do is figure out how *you* can do this best. Look at what others are doing, and learn all you can about what's available by way of equipment and tools. You're not obligated to own or use any particular thing. Your filing tools can be folders and file cabinets or boxes, drawers, shelves, piles, or file pockets on the wall. Not to mention the never-ending possibilities of filing on computer. Likewise, filing doesn't just mean papers and notes and documents. We don't all work with paper only. Some of us need to file samples, parts, paint chips, patterns, plant specimens, artwork, tools, bottles, or books, as well. But when it comes down to the bottom line, you need to adapt everything to your own way of thinking and doing things.

When you set up things, remember that you want your files to be out of your knock-over space, but also convenient, so that you can clamp onto what you need in an instant.

There are a few more secrets of filing I've learned (and use), after forty years of watching the finest filers.

1. Focus on WHY First

You can't hit a nontarget. Most people can't decide what to keep because they haven't really focused on why they're keeping it. It's easy to wander or get lost on a journey with no destination. So think first about what you want and where you're going. List your main goals, the things you want to accomplish in your job and career (and if this is your home office, your life, home, family, organizations, hobbies, etc.). This will give you your main categories. Then make and mark a place for each of them. Think, too, about what you will want or need to collect for each of them. Once you do this, the rest is just mechanical.

2. Reduce

Reduce what you're filing; condense it. Pick up that pile of To Be Filed and peel it, pare it down, lessen the load. This is the ultimate secret of filing and of finding things in the files.

Get rid of any duplicates or unreadables or envelopes or packaging. Don't stash the whole catalog when ballpoint pens or gummed labels are the only things you're interested in. Remove just those pages and the order blanks and chuck the other 112 pages. Don't keep the whole magazine, just the article you really want. Don't keep the whole 35-page report when only 2 pages pertain to your project or area. In things like this, covers, binders, and ads are ¾ of the bulk. Get rid of them, and keep the meat. Don't keep all the brochures and handouts the salesperson gave you if there's only one thing you'd ever buy from her. Keep only the salesperson's business card, and write the name and serial number of the item on the back. Unless you intend to use it right away, don't keep information (such as special sale offers) when you'll automatically receive updates and fresh, new ones whether you want them or not.

For that matter, are you sure you need to file it at all? As one office manager emphasized to me, "If only we weren't so hooked on thinking we need to keep things, just because they have good information or might make a good reference. Maybe we just need to *read* them. Many 'filed' things are never, ever looked at again until it's time to 'clean out the files.'"

One Piece Instead of Ten!
(Design Your Own Paper Reducers)

Publicity work is a record-keeping nightmare—the paperwork multiplies like bacteria and there isn't enough time or file space to hold and control all the things you need to have at your fingertips.

When I first started writing, I knew nothing about media, but I learned fast when I went out on the road doing five or six TV and radio shows and newspaper interviews every day for weeks in a row. There were nine kinds of important information that my staff needed to have handy, so one day I designed a form that would put it all on a single page, in exactly the way that suited our needs. It greatly simplified the whole process, from scheduling to follow-up to filing, eliminated all the wondering as well as paper, and took only seconds to fill out. We started this twenty years ago and it's become an asset you wouldn't believe. When a station calls, we can pull their record and within seconds know where they are and what I did there before, and when—as well as what kind of response it got. We love the sheet and so do the media people.

You can boil down your own paperwork for your own purposes. Take a dozen things you'd be filing and handling separately, all the information you have to give and receive about something, and invent a form that fits all twelve things on it. Then you can use a single 8½" × 11" sheet for it all instead of boxes, folders, etc.

Who do you think makes up forms anyway—people like *you* make the best ones, because you know exactly what you need and what it's all for and how it fits together. This is fun, fast, and will lighten your load so much, you'll wonder why you didn't do it sooner.

If you're using conventional filing furniture, try to standardize your forms and correspondence—or convert everything to 8½" × 11"–sized sheet. If you toss tiny little scraps or snippets of paper in a file, for example, they get lost or stray. And if you try to cram big stuff into a regular-size file, it gets crushed and wrinkled. I always tape small stuff onto an 8½" × 11"–sized sheet. Most oversize things can be reduced on a copier, trimmed, folded in half neatly *when you first go to file them,* or cut up and pasted onto 8½" × 11"–sized sheets.

3. Group Filing

Group filing is always faster than one little piece at a time. Note that the chef waits until the meat, potatoes, and vegetables are all together before he serves them, rather than bringing out each one individually. I find it twice as effective to toss file-ables into an I.P. (Important Paper) file. Let them collect and "ferment" in there a few days; then pick out a whole box of fileables, and do it all in one motion. Plus, after fermenting, some of the stuff in there proves to be chaff, and so your filing is further reduced.

Likewise, when you're filing a big pile of stuff, wait till you've sorted all the way to the bottom of the pile before you start filing anything. Better to make just one trip to drop all the new stuff into your "Aardvarks" and "Iguanas" files, rather than five or six.

4. You'll Pay for Poor Naming

Should this be filed under P, N, or F? You can start your file labels with any word you want, make them as unique and quirky as you want, if they're strictly your files (it'll be harder for anyone else to find the hot stuff that way, too). But if they're "public" files that others must use, use the most obvious and logical word—and pray.

5. Fit the Pockets to the Potential
. . . Right from the Start

Many paper-organizing setups end up being too small. You know what I mean; it's happened to us all since childhood. The pail is too small for all the tadpoles we want to bring home, the vase is too small for all the flowers we picked, and our pocket is too small for all the marbles we won. Likewise, in the office, we often come up with a neat idea for keeping, storing, or organizing something, and the concept is just right and it works. And like anything else that works, we use it like crazy, and suddenly that drawer or cabinet or whatever is stuffed too full. Then that excellent means of clutter control just becomes more clutter.

I started a "Grandkids" drawer in my office at home, for example, and it worked great for the first one or two grandkids, but by the time I had fifteen, it was a scrunched and overflowing mess that I'd insisted on continuing because it worked so well originally.

Remember this when you're setting up things, right at the beginning. Allow room for expansion, more than you think you'll need now, so the good things will always have space. When you run out of room, it'll always be at the wrong time and place and you'll end up with a mess you hate to face.

6. Color

Color-coding can be a great filing tool and organizer. My editor uses felt-tip pens for the purpose, which seemed silly to me until a manuscript came back and anything marked with red meant questions that needed answering, orange meant copy that had to be repositioned, yellow highlighting called out artwork ideas for the artist, and so on. Other people use different colors of paper stock for different projects, to speed sorting and finding. Just be sure to define your color scheme clearly before you start, and don't switch hues midstream.

Some people use different colored paper for different projects the way some homeowners use different colored sheets for different beds—it makes it easier for things to end up in the right place.

My Own Filing Formula

I have an extensive filing system in my office at home, not just for my half-dozen businesses and scores of Scout, church, and civic projects, but the several hundred articles and at least sixty books I have underway. I also have an almost constant flow of media interviews and public appearances, and I'm on the road about 150 days a year with business travel, speaking, and performing. People ask me all the time, "How can you keep track of all this?" and once I explain and show them, they realize it's ultrasimple.

I may be doing sixty books, but I've been working on them over the last ten years. I finish a few each year and start five more. I'm writing parts and pieces of them all the time. And when I'm out and about anywhere, anytime, and I have an idea for one of them or something crops up in conversation or in a paper, magazine, or movie relating to any of my books, I save it. For example, right now I'm doing books on solving our country's big, embarrassing "litter" problem, on making cleaning easier for the physically handicapped, how to recapture the joy of life, the real secrets of personal organization, my own guide to business management, how to build a rock fence, how to be a better grandpa, and my autobiography. There's always material there for the taking; all we have to do is write it down, rip it out, take a picture of it, or whatever. Some days I find and collect fifty things to keep and use and share.

Being a drawer man, I don't like file folders much. I like to have things laid out right in front of me—it helps me visualize things, and that's the way I want it. So I bought a bunch of those metal cabinets with lots of little drawers (available at office supply stores), and now I have 120 drawers behind my desk, all labeled with titles and topics. I just bring my pile of notes and clippings home, and when I'm too tired to do anything else, I take five or ten minutes and drop each one into the proper drawer. (Since they're drawers rather than hanging files, I can fit books and booklets I want to save for reference right in there too.) That's it! I know where things are and they're easy to get to—that's the heart of filing.

> Filing is a good thing to do in "tired time."

Sometimes I'll just keep dropping stuff into a drawer for five or six years and never take it out. Then when I have what I think is enough material for a book, I find a day alone and dump the drawer in the middle of my office floor, sort it into chapters, and then tape all the fragments into order. In just a couple of hours, I have a good basic book skeleton that just has to be expanded, typed, organized a little more, and edited. My file has art and cover ideas, too, and even format ideas I've seen and liked.

I've learned in my life not to wait until you need something to go after it. Do it right as you go along, as life goes on, every day, anywhere you are, and then FILE it.

For the more immediate projects I have seriously underway (usually around twenty or so), I cut down some cardboard boxes until they're about five inches deep and then label them on the front: "TV segments," "Eureka," "Kangaroo Kart," "Educate the User," "My Autobiography," "New Girls Camp," etc., and then line up all the boxes on the top of tables around my desk. (I know they make those pesky stacking trays for things like this, but if I can't see the top of the pile, I get insecure.)

Notes Old and New

You can't dig through any pile of paper anywhere without finding notes and notes and notes. Every day, every single one of us makes notes, and we sure exercise creativity in capturing those thoughts, that information! If we don't have a pad or notebook with us, we do it on the backs of programs or business cards, on folders, envelopes, boxes, napkins, shirt cuffs, or the margins of our check register. We jot down a word, a name, a measurement, or a sentence because we want to be sure to keep it, and don't want to take a chance of losing it by just trying to remember it.

This gathering process is important, but after all the gobbling up comes the indigestion. How do we assimilate it all? Most of us have tons of notes taken at important meetings or events, or even just our own personal thoughts and inspirations about all kinds of things . . . piled and heaped or lost and buried somewhere.

Like many of you, I don't go anywhere, even to bed or to the backwoods, without a pen or pencil and paper. I average over 100 notes a day—good stuff from good sources, real cream, such as the key thoughts scooped off the top of a long sermon or from a stimulating conversation. This is all stuff that I want to keep and use, but I learned long ago that the keeping is the easy part. It's the using that requires the smarts. We've all had the perfect word or quote or saying—somewhere. We know we did write it down and save it; we know we do have it somewhere . . . but we can't find it. This is pure agony and a total waste of time and life. If you can't find it and use it, then it has no value at all. It's just insulation for the office, fuel for a good office fire, or more clutter on the computer.

Process Notes Quickly . . . Now!

You have only one choice when it comes to notes. You've got to file them while they're fresh—daily, or at least weekly— or they're worthless. Never stack a note. The minute you get back, or the day you get home, file the note or enter it into your computer, print it out, and file it. Then you'll have it. If you ever pile it, you'll just keep on doing so and in a year or two have piles and boxes of notes you couldn't sort or use in the rest of your lifetime. Saving for a later, better time is pure fantasy. "Later" never really comes in life. Later is now. Today is the day that matters and today is when you need to do something with those notes or they won't matter later.

When I attended college, I also ran a full-scale business, built and maintained a home, fathered five children, played sports, belonged to the debate team, was an officer in campus organizations, a member of the Army National Guard, and handled several administrative and teaching jobs at church. All of this, including all those classes, meant pages and pages and pages of notes, often taken fast and sloppily and with primitive spelling and abbreviations. But by golly, if I took the time to gather them, I was determined to use them. So I forced myself to develop a system, my own note-processing system (which each and every one of us has to do or paper wins and we lose).

In the evening, after all the kids were in bed, I laid out all my notes and sorted them and typed them on 8½″ × 11″ sheets. Then, right then, I filed or bound them together. It was amazing how fast I could type up a whole day's notes, and the act of typing them was a great way to reinforce and memorize what was said there. This speeded up studying for exams, too. A few minutes of running my eyes over those neatly summarized notes and I had it.

My greatest pleasure when doing this was to slip a couple of pieces of carbon paper in when I was doing class notes and take them with me to class the next day. Then when someone who'd missed the last session was panicking, I'd hand him or her a fresh, neat, complete set of notes. It blew them away. It didn't cost me a thing and boy did I gain friends.

Having notes lost or jumbled somewhere in a pile, file, or even computer is as bad as not having them at all. Prompt and regular upkeep is the only way. Only you know how your brain train runs—find a way to expedite note processing that fits it. Get those notes translated and sorted and put them right where they belong. Do it now and do it daily.

I could tell you not to take so many notes, but that's like saying don't get hungry or huffy. You can cut it down a little, though—don't take notes on everything, just the best stuff, the stuff you really need to record or remember. And don't bother to transcribe and keep notes you don't really need or want, even if you did dutifully take them at the time to keep yourself awake or look busy. You also may not need notes when someone is already supplying a summary in handy, concise printed form—you could just languish in the luxury of *listening*.

Chapter 11
Desk for Success:
Design Clutter Out

One of the largest hotels in Chicago is directly across a narrow street from one of the largest glass-fronted offices in town. I've stayed in this hotel several times, and when you're on the fifteenth floor, that all-glass office is dead center out the window, like a giant visual aid of office anatomy, over 800 offices at a glance. It's like an anthill cutaway and much more intriguing to watch than the soaps or the sitcoms on TV. There are 800 different screens, and some have one main character, while some have five bosses and assistants all thrashing around. Some are being cleaned, some are vacant with all the gadgets left to run the office by themselves. There are 800 different styles and arrangements of desks and other furniture, shelves, files, and decorations. Some of the occupants are floor stackers, some are shelf stackers, and believe it or not (I'd never noticed this much before) many are carriers. They carry papers and things around all the time, like a security blanket. Some are in their offices starting work at 4:30 A.M., and others are there until 2:30 A.M. finishing. Some leave for lunch, some stay and eat at their desks, and some work right through the middle of the day. Some are paper hiders, others paper displayers; some seem to have too much to do, others not enough.

Every time I see this, it confirms my own conclusion that there is no right or best or perfect workspace—only what is best or perfect for you.

A workspace designed to fit *you* is even more important than just the right clothes or the perfect vehicle. Many of us spend more waking hours in the office than we do at home, and what we manage to accomplish—or not accomplish—at work often has more of an effect on our entire life than any other single thing.

If you've ever seen the cockpit of an airplane, you know that it's all there, precisely fitted to the pilot who sits in the middle of it all with everything in the right place and rhythm to get the job done. Think about this for your workspace, present or future. Design it for use and fit it to you—that will help keep it clutter-free. Yes, I do know that most of us are led into a cubicle or a room with a desk (and sometimes even some furniture) and told, "Here it is, work away!" But this isn't the only workspace you'll ever have, and it isn't forever, and it isn't the way it has to stay. If you are convinced you can do something better, most bosses with any sense will give you a chance to try.

There might be standards and rules you have to observe at work, sizes and schedules you have to work within, but the strategy and function should be up to you or adjusted to you where it needs to be.

Buy and build, design, change, and fix your workplace so that it truly fits the jobs and projects you use it for. There must be 106,421 different types of desks, chairs, credenzas, calendars, phones, cabinets, and computers for the office these days. If you're short, tall, long-armed, short-armed, nearsighted, or farsighted, you should fix the office to fit you.

Many years ago now, knowing nothing about the adjustable ("tilt") steering wheels that had just come out in the new cars, I drove a rental car from Salt Lake City to Los Angeles with the wheel folded up against the dashboard, where the last driver had left it when he got out. Everyone got a big laugh at the arm cramps and sore back I got in the process, but even I have to admit how great it is that when you get into an auto to drive now, you can adjust not just the steering wheel but mirrors, seats, and belts to fit you instantly.

How much more important is this at work, making things fit you and your style of doing things, rather than just accepting and using any old system.

Cut Your Own Pattern

It is your workspace—and there's no one on this earth just like you. If you have a desk, you've probably lived long enough to formulate your very own ways of doing things. You also have your own values, your own likes, dislikes, and schedules. For sure no one has a life, business, or office pattern just like yours. My own or anyone else's exact methods may not fit your situation.

For example, there are those of us who can remember every detail of everything we touch or come in contact with. Others of us have about a five-minute retention and retrieval capacity—we have to have everything written down and labeled. Some of us like to work on one job or project at a time, finish it, and move on. Others, on the more impetuous side (like me), have sixty or seventy projects going all at once. We may both accomplish the same number of things by the year's end, but our process is different, and hence our desktop, tables, files, and tools will be. It's not a question of good or bad, just different. I like to leave all my active projects out in sight, in piles, and so does my editor and many others. Yet many of you are happier just picking the project of the hour out of a big drawer full of files with big clear labels.

To me those Rolodex files are among the biggest nuisances that ever sat on a desktop. Ugly, awkward, and usually outdated, I took mine home and let the grandkids use it as a spin-toy. But many highly effective people swear by them.

Some of those weekly, monthly, daily, etc., planners, and Palm Pilots, for instance, are nothing but a mass of confusion to me. But some of my most efficient employees say they do wonders to help you organize and discipline yourself.

So shrug off any guilt you may feel for not following others' organization plans or concepts. You think differently, and you don't need to do it like anyone else.

Make Sure Your Office System Fits You, Too

Take a hard look at the size and height and location and placement of things. Everything in your work area, from where the files are located to where you set your briefcase to where the wastebasket is, should fit your physical and mental flow, not just what's "always done." Be bold enough to design or adjust your area of operations so that it truly fits you. Even if someone else thinks it's weird, it'll make you more comfortable and productive and help keep things clean and uncluttered, too.

Keep your eye out for systems that suit you, and adapt them. Tailor your tools and furnishings to your height, weight, temperament, schedule, operation size, and situation. Borrow all kinds of ideas, try them on, and use the ones that fit your measurements. No one owns organization, though some "efficiency experts" might create that impression. The bottom line is these are just tools—only you can make them work.

Learn from others, but don't just copy what they do. Adapt what fits your flow and feels good to you. Look for ideas that fit your patterns and ways of doing things. When you see them, grab them!

> Find and get and use what truly suits you, and
> you'll collect less clutter and get more done.

There's something to love at first sight. Often you'll see something in use somewhere that just fits you and what you want and need. Right then, not later, look for the label and the manufacturer and call or send for information. Or find out where it came from. More likely than not, the proud owner will be glad to rustle up the data for you.

You may think you have all the office catalogs on earth, but no, there are hundreds more. Check the Internet or reference guides to mail-order companies at your local library. And there are usually specialty stores in the larger towns and cities that have more than your local office supply stores. If you can't find what you want and need in all this, then build it (as long as your building manager says it's okay!). Even if you have to use an old door and two retired nail kegs to make the kind of table you want, or convert an old refrigerator into a file cabinet.

Chapter 12
The Case for Office TLC

The following is a true story, and it happened in the head-quarters of one of our country's premium companies. The fifth floor was the executive floor, the place where the big wheels rolled out the rules and routines by which the whole place was run, and it had the most and best furniture and equipment and decorations. Naturally, the company wanted these offices to look exquisite all the time.

Now, it may surprise you to know that big bosses like this are not always quite so big on neatness and cleanliness. So, to compensate for any of the inhabitants' shortcomings in this area (their tendency to leave their office in a deplorable condition at times), we often assigned our best custodian to serve that section of the building. In this case it was Tina, a shy woman who had more than twenty-five years of experience in office cleaning, and getting down to the bottom line, she was the best.

One of these executives not quite as good at housekeeping as he was in "Operations" was the top man, T. E. Dirtydesk (T. E., we were sure, stood for Toss Everywhere). As it is in life, so it is in offices—what the boss does the junior executives follow. T. E. inspired a lot of messiness beyond his own door, down the office row. Lack of neatness wasn't T. E.'s only negative, either. Cleaning people had a pretty low status with him, and he certainly didn't ever worry about using the words "please" or "thank you" with them. Our heroine Tina had cleaned his and all the other executive offices every evening for fifteen years—wiping, dusting, polishing, dumping the left-behind coffee or soggy cigar butts, rounding up scattered magazines, vacuuming the fingernail clippings off the carpet, rounding up the papers and wrappers that missed the basket, dumping and shining up the grimy ashtrays, and spending hours removing carelessly created stains.

Tina was invisible to T. E., and to Tina (who had seen T. E. only a few times when he was working late), he was an inconsiderate slob. They never spoke or even blinked on the rare occasion when they passed each other.

The energy crisis hit the country about then, and this company, being a leading corporation very much in the public view, made a dramatic gesture to reduce energy costs. They went to "day cleaning," which meant that instead of us janitors cleaning from 4:00 P.M. until midnight, with 10,000 lights on and the heat up, we cleaned while the tenants were still in

their offices. That went for T. E.'s turf, too. Cleaning T. E.'s crumb-bedecked office was bad enough, but now Tina had to spend time in a room with him as well. His office was an inescapable duty to her, and she was a necessary evil to him, nothing more.

Finally she, the best in the business, began to break under the strain—she dreaded his desk and office more each day. Then when all was about to be lost, a miracle! One afternoon, as usual, she cleaned around him, dumping baskets and dusting double-time to get out of there as quickly as she could. When her eye fell on a freshly hung picture of a junior soccer team, she broke her fifteen-year silence and blurted out, "Why do you have this picture?" T. E. jumped up, hustled over to the wall, and pointing a big nicotine-stained finger at one of the meek little players in the back row, said, "That's my grandson." Equally enthusiastic, Tina pointed her finger at a young man in the front line. "That's *my* grandson!" T. E. was not unaware that that little gentleman *was* the soccer team—the brilliant team leader. "You're kidding," he said. "He's plenty good, too," she added proudly. "He sure is," T. E. agreed. That was it. She and her little cleaning cart were gone for the day, but that moment changed not only those two but numerous others in the end. For a magic thing called communication had happened, and they each realized the other was human.

The next day, when Tina whisked in to clean, the magazines were straight and there was no paper on the floor. So the next visit she did some extra things. The day after that, she noticed there was no coffee in the trash basket and the ashtrays were all dumped, so she brought and left a nice bouquet of flowers. The next day T. E. happened to be off on a business trip, and Tina was amazed—his desk was immaculate and there tucked neatly underneath it was a can of desk cleaner and a cloth. So she cleaned and conditioned his leather chair.

No, they didn't end up getting married, but as far as I'm concerned something even better happened. T. E., with only a tiny bit of effort, cut the cleaning needs in his office way down and what's more, he *felt better* about his office and his work. Then, believe it or not, he called a meeting of all the managers under him and informed them that they had the best, kindest, sweetest cleaner in the whole United States doing their office, so they better keep and leave it immaculate, pick up after themselves in the cafeteria, and no more *Wall Street Journals* on the floor by the toilets, etc. With just a few words he raised the consciousness and level of "clean" by at least 80 percent. Tina had so little to do, she added another whole area to her schedule, saving the company a bundle of money, to boot.

Cleaning Doesn't Cost Just the Company

It costs you—personally. Cleaning and repair are a big part of overhead, which is money you might get if it weren't "poured down the toilet." The boss may own the office space, but you pay directly for the maintenance of it. Every cost of cleaning, from chewing gum removal to plastic liners for the trash cans, comes from the operational budget, which is the same bottom line that's figured to see if you get raises—or for that matter keep your job. Few bosses are greedy; most of them are smart enough to share the profits with you whenever they can, and the less expense, the more profit. An extra person just to clean "slob stuff" in an office, stuff we really ought to take care of ourselves, but we leave for the "cleaning people" instead, costs about more than $10,000 a year, counting labor and supplies. If we all spent just five minutes a day to help keep our own area clean, that money could be dropped into the Profit column instead of Expense, making some raises (or maybe bonus money) possible.

Many people misunderstand a janitor's duty—janitors aren't there to be anyone's personal maid or valet; we're hired and assigned to service the facility. We polish desks, disinfect, maintain the hard floors and carpets, clean the toilets, and dump the waste receptacles, but it's not our job to round up all the loose papers everywhere, or wash everyone's snack dishes. Nor is it our job to move and sort through and rearrange things in your desk and office so that we can find them to service them. It's the personal, individual job of each and every one of us to pick up, put up, and organize our own area and articles.

I've written cleaning specs for some of the world's largest and best companies, and here is the clause in the average pro cleaning contract that covers your desk and office:

Varsity Contractors, Inc., will dust, spot clean, and service all clear, available surfaces in the office area. We will not move or interfere with material in, on, or around the area.

In other words, if people want us to clean, the area has to be left accessible so that there's no chance we will damage or disturb anything. Few office workers know this. Many times, thousands of times every night, in fact, someone responsible for caring for an area stands in front of a desk or an office and wonders, *How far should I go?* The next morning, the office owner or inhabitant stands in front of the same things wondering what (if anything) the #*@&%*!! cleaner did. I myself hate to have anyone touch anything on or around my desk. So I keep it clean, and they don't have to.

What's the best way to communicate with the janitor or the office cleaner when you have some special cleaning problem or request, or need a little extra help with trash detail or whatever in conjunction with your decluttering campaign? Leave a note in the middle of your desk with a polite written request—signed and dated. (And a thank-you note when it's done.)

Taking the responsibility for cleaning your own personal area and property isn't just sensible and a money and energy saver for the company or your own business, or anywhere, it's a nothing less than noble action. It always makes us feel good to know we didn't dump on someone else. When I tell people that before I leave my room in any hotel or motel, I always take a few seconds to spiff it up—wipe out the sink, pick up the towels, and straighten the place up—they always laugh and call me a clean freak. Then I ask them how much they're usually willing to spend to "feel good." In this case I can feel good about myself all day for next to nothing. Many people I know do this, too, and have joined the "Neatnik Club" to feel better about themselves. Membership costs only a minute or two a day at your desk, shop, or studio.

The best part of this self-clean, keep clean campaign is that it creates a spirit and standard that helps to repel and prevent future cluttering by you or others.

Trash Can Manners

We seem to have the idea that once we get anything into a wastebasket, it's taken care of, gone, and we've done right. Not quite! Chewed gum tossed into a receptacle or onto a surface of any kind, for example, is true toxic waste. It sticks to anything it comes up against, and then it has to be pried, scraped, wrestled, or soaked with solvent to get rid of it. So wrapping that little wad with paper when you're finished with it is a wise (and thoughtful) idea. Same with food. People often toss a piece of cake into a nice office wastebasket and the frosting smears all over the sides and bottom of the can, hardening there and tripling cleaning time, as well as attracting insects.

> What does the office janitor hate the most? All of those throws that miss the wastebasket when it's only six inches from our knees!

Dropped clips, coins, tacks, and rubber bands often roll out of reach, so we leave them "for the cleaning people." (After all, that's what they get paid for.) Often the cleaners are as careless as the droppers, and a $400 vacuum is soon in the repair shop.

The Office Care Kit

I keep a little kit in the bottom drawer of my desk, sort of an office care and repair kit. With this it takes only a couple of seconds a day to keep my desk and work area perfect, and I can catch any spills immediately (if you wait till later you may have a permanent stain). Here's what I have in my kit:

- A couple of microfiber or terry cleaning cloths
- Disposable treated dustcloths, such as Masslinn

- A spray bottle filled with a mild all-purpose cleaner solution (You can get a professional-strength spray bottle, and little packets of cleaner you mix up yourself with water, from a janitorial-supply store; or make friends with the janitor.)
- Disposable premoistened towelettes
- The Eureka Mighty Mite, a handy little vacuum to have around the office (It's small enough to store compactly and strong enough to really do something. And it'll last a good, long time if it's used just around the office.)
- Minivacuum attachments (They are just right for office machines and all of their intricate little dirt traps, including keyboards. They fit just right on a Mighty Mite.)

If you don't want to round all this up, we'll put a complete kit together for you. Send an e-mail to *don@aslett.com* or write to:

Don Aslett Office Kit
PO Box 700-O
Pocatello, ID 83204

The Pride and Pleasure of Polishing Up the Finer Things ... Yourself!

If you have the fortune of inhabiting an office or workspace wherein you have some fine personal treasures, you know that things like this are generally not in the regular cleaning schedule. I'm talking about those things made of brass or chrome, genuine leather, fine wood or fine fabric—those antiques and collector's items and other special furnishings that require some extra skill and attention. Hired help often doesn't have the expertise or the assignment to maintain them. They may be dusted or wiped down once in a while, but they're seldom or never really cleaned, polished, or conditioned unless you make special arrangements for it to be done or do it yourself.

There's great satisfaction in doing it yourself, as anyone who's ever curried his favorite horse or polished her antique car knows. I'm going to give you the basics of what to do and how to do it, and most of it takes only minutes. Don't let it go! Fine metal oxidizes and fine wood and leather dry out. Offices today are full of dust and other airborne pollutants. Hands have not only skin oil and traces of all the lotions and potions we've used recently, but bacteria, too. All this transfers to anything people touch, and even to what they don't.

First, the Wood

At least 95 percent of the wood in any office is "sealed" or coated with a clear protective finish such as varnish, polyurethane, or lacquer. We pro cleaners call this a "membrane finish." It means you don't have to worry about moisture hurting the wood when you're cleaning it, because for the most part the cleaning solution or polish never touches the actual wood. This is true of most wood paneling, desks and other furniture, and even floors.

All office wood should be dusted regularly. You have three great dusting choices:

- Microfiber cloth that you can use dry or damp
- A feather duster made with real ostrich feathers like the Texas Feather Duster
- Disposable Masslinn cloths (available at janitorial supply stores)

Bear in mind that you'll find the worst and most dust in the "Low Zone" about three feet from the floor down. So go after all that dust on the chair legs and rungs, the base of the table, etc.

Office wood should occasionally be damp-wiped to remove handprints, smudges, flyspecks, food drips or spills, and residue from things set on or leaned against it. Dampen (don't drench!) a microfiber or terry cleaning cloth in a solution of oil soap such as Wood Wash or Murphy Oil Soap, or any gentle cleaner, and wipe the surface twice—once quickly to wet it, and the second time to remove the loosened soil. Then, before the dampness even has a chance to evaporate, polish the surface dry immediately with a clean cotton towel.

This will bring back the original luster and give a much cleaner and better looking result than piling on oils and polishes the way most people do. Just don't allow the dampness to sit on the wood long, and remember to dry-buff with the grain of the wood.

This damp-wipe/quick-dry process can even be used on antique wood, and in fact almost anything in the office, even upholstery (you don't want to do any wet cleaning of electronic equipment, of course). Just use the same technique with the cleaning solution you'd normally use on that item.

Every few years, or after a move, remodeling project, or fire, wood paneling may need to be washed, and this constitutes a major cleanup. Get two buckets, one empty and one half-full of a solution of a mild (neutral) detergent or oil soap in warm water. Take a sponge and dip it only about a quarter inch into the solution and wet down about a 4' × 4' section of the area you want to clean. Work from top to bottom and go over it twice, once to wet the surface and loosen the soil and the second time to remove the loosened soil. Now *quickly* dry the wood with microfiber or terry toweling, wiping with the grain. Then squeeze the sponge into the empty bucket and all that soil you removed will be gone, instead of muddying up your cleaning water! Now repeat the process. Each time do about as much as you can comfortably reach before it dries.

On any wall, stubborn marks from chair bumps, handles, or other things can be removed safely by rubbing gently with a soft (white) nylon pad. Just make sure you wet it before you scrub with it. Never use harsh chemicals or cleansers or abrasive scrub pads—you'll end up with a dull, scuffed spot.

A good cleaning as just described will take off all the old, sticky, gummy layers of wax and polish, but it may leave the surface a little dull. If you insist on a shine and would like to add a little extra protection, then apply furniture polish—*conservatively*. Pick a polish and then stay with that same brand and type. Most of us switch around, and many polishes and waxes are incompatible (some are oil based, some silicone, etc.). The result is ugly streaks and white patches.

For Other Hard Surfaces

For metal, plastic laminate ("Formica"), glass, fiberglass, vinyl, chrome, even computer housings, keep a little spray bottle of mild all-purpose cleaner solution in your desk. Don't spray surfaces directly with it—there's too much risk of overspray or drips. Take a soft microfiber or cotton cloth and spray a little solution onto one side of it. Then wipe with the dampened side, and turn the cloth over and wipe and polish dry with the other. You can use the cloth over and over this way, then when it gets grimy, take it home and wash and dry it—and away you go again. Paper towels or rags don't work nearly as well; they leave a lot of lint.

Leather

It's nice, and it lasts and lasts, but it does stain and get dirty. Leather furniture should be vacuumed or dusted regularly just like other upholstered furniture, and cleaned when it begins to get soiled. You can do this with saddle soap, following the directions that come with it and being sure to use moisture sparingly. If leather seems to be getting dry, use a leather conditioner on it after cleaning.

Upholstery

To really clean fine upholstery, you need to hire a seasoned pro with professional extracting equipment. To help keep those heavy-use armrest and headrest areas clean meanwhile, sponge on some foam from a good upholstery shampoo or even a Woolite solution; then rub it in and blot it dry with clean terry towels. This will pull out much of the dirt and grease (even if it does leave a little detergent residue, which the next full-scale shampooing will remove).

Brass/Silver/Copper

These and other metals on fixtures, decorations, and artwork will gradually tarnish or "oxidize," developing a dull, dark, cloudy surface. If it's something that looks nicely antiqued or classy with a tarnished finish (called *verdigris* on copper, for example), you're in luck—just leave it as is. Otherwise, you'll want to use metal polish. Use the right kind for the metal in question, and take it easy with it: most metal polishes are abrasive, and every time you use them you're removing a tiny bit of the surface of the metal. The best way to proceed here is to apply a tiny bit of polish to a soft cotton cloth and wipe it on. Allow it to sit on there a few seconds; then with another clean, dry soft cloth, rub and polish the metal back to its original luster. When there isn't much more "black" coming off on the polishing cloth and the object shines, that's good enough. Using a little dropcloth around the object while you're polishing is a bright idea!

Some people lacquer their tarnishable metals—I wouldn't do this unless it's in a high-use location such as on a door. Many lamps, etc., are lacquered right at the factory. Don't use metal polish or any strong cleaner or scrubbing action on a lacquered finish—just dust and damp-wipe with all-purpose cleaner solution as needed.

Oil Paintings

Oil paintings do gradually get dirty. If that lovely little landscape set you or your boss back a pretty penny to buy it, I'd leave the cleaning of it to an expert, of course. The safest and easiest way to clean oil paintings otherwise is with a soft rubber pad called a dry sponge. You just whisk it over the surface, and like a gentle eraser it will pull all the dust and dirt right off. You never use water with it. When both sides of the dry sponge are heavily soiled, you just throw it away and start a new one.

Professionals use these by the gross to clean smoked-up walls, and they're also a good way to clean expensive wall coverings, acoustic tile, cork, and other nonwashable surfaces in your office. Dry sponges can be hard to find (many paint stores and janitorial-supply stores have them), but they're inexpensive. I keep a good supply of them on hand, so e-mail me at *don@aslett.com* or write to me at the address on page 203 if you can't find any locally.

Glassed Wall Hangings

When cleaning the glassed fronts of framed pictures, photos, certificates, mirrors, etc., never spray them directly— the solution could run down inside, or in the case of mirrors, run to the edges and damage the backing. Spray some glass cleaner onto a soft, clean cloth and then use it to shine the surface.

Computers

Electronic equipment and especially computers are pretty thin-skinned when it comes to cleanliness. They seem to draw dust, dirt, and lint like a magnet. And all of this, plus the fallout from us human operators—hair, dandruff, spilled food and liquid, crumbs—can harm or even destroy them. Real vigilance is called for here. Keeping units covered when they're not in use (yes, even in a nice office) does help.

So first, dust regularly with one of my favorite dusters:

- A microfiber cloth (dry or dampened with water)
- A feather duster made with real ostrich feathers like the Texas Feather Duster
- Disposable Masslinn cloths

To remove the stuff that gets in the cracks of keyboards and other equipment you can get a set of little attachments for a canister vacuum (Eureka's Mighty Mite is perfect) that can do all the necessary sucking and blowing. Cans of compressed air (complete with extension tubes to reach the smallest crack) are also available anywhere that sells computer supplies.

Our hands are often sticky, from skin oil or hand lotion or whatever we just had for lunch. So keeping some premoistened towelettes in the drawer to wipe immediately when we need to will keep things fresh and pleasant and prevent hardened slicks (and repair bills) later.

Keyboard wipes (available from computer suppliers) will clean grimy keys, as will cotton swabs moistened lightly with a mild cleaning solution.

When a keyboard does get really dirty you can wash it. Experts taught me the right way to do this. First vacuum and blow out the keyboard thoroughly; then mix up a little neutral cleaner solution and whip it well to get some foam. Unplug the keyboard and hold it upside down, then dip a soft toothbrush in the foam and apply it sparingly to the face of the keys, scrubbing gently as needed to loosen dirt and grunge; then dry with a soft cotton cloth. Leave it upside down till it's good and dry, so that if a drop or two of moisture should happen to remain it won't run down into the electronics.

Epigraph
The Rewards of Less Mess

I don't have to tell you that a cluttered desk, cubicle, workspace, or office will get attention. Problem is, it's mainly irritation and pity. The biggest reward of all for cleaning up your clutter will be positive attention, praise and raises, plus a new sense of efficiency and pride. You may be the exact same person as ever, but your new environment will present you much more powerfully and positively to be loved, needed, respected. You'll notice an upgrade in not just your image and speed but people's confidence in you.

A whole bunch of things will happen when you come clean:

1. **You'll feel good,** and feeling good is everything. The money we spend and the things we do (traveling, eating, buying, playing, and imbibing) in an attempt to feel good are almost ridiculous. Here, for the expenditure of just a little effort, you can and will feel good every single day—when you're coming to work, while you're there, and when you leave. What a high—and it doesn't cost a dime.

2. **You'll feel a secret surge of confidence.** We all see and feel this in people who have removed the (pack) rat's nest from their place. They act differently now; they have a sense of control where they were always bogged in confusion before.

3. **You'll welcome new experiences and opportunities.** Think of how you feel at home when the whole house is squared away, kids clean, hedges trimmed, yard mowed, and someone you like and respect shows up at the door. A spirit of "Come on in" floods your soul. On the other hand, when there are dirty dishes, unmade beds, dropped popcorn, newspapers, and night clothes scattered all over, and the cat just missed the litter box, the sudden appearance of a visitor strikes terror in your heart.

   A clean office doesn't just welcome, it beckons, not only to your boss and customers and colleagues, but new assignments and opportunities. Because it says "I'm ready."

4. **You'll have room to grow.** What a good feeling it is to have room for more—in our stomach, our shopping bag, freezer, file cabinet, guest room, garden, or hard disk. A place for more, the unexpected, is always so satisfying. You never know what new thing might pop up or come along. And being ready by having room is a real secret of winning. Jammed, overloaded drawers, files, spaces, and closets leave no room, physically or mentally, for new,

more, or better opportunities. Where do you set (or do you even dare?) an important message or assignment on a junked desk? We always hesitate, for fear they won't find it in the heap, or will lose it.

5. **It'll save all those apologies.** Have you ever noticed how much of our lives are spent apologizing and making excuses to cushion questionable conditions or behavior? No more! A spiffy office speaks fast and well.

6. (And a nice little extra here.) **We, the janitors, will love you forever!**

About the Author

Don Aslett is "America's #1 Cleaner," and cleaning is his business. The professional cleaning company he founded more than forty-five years ago, Varsity Contractors, is among the biggest and best in the industry today. And the dozens of books on cleaning and home care he's written in the last decade have sold more than 3 million copies and made him a household word to Americans.

He became the founder and guru of the decluttering movement in 1984 with the publication of *Clutter's Last Stand*—the first book ever to deal with our desperate need to dejunk our homes and our lives, and still the bible of dejunkers everywhere. The sequel he did by popular demand in 1991, *Not for Packrats Only*—a detailed guide to home decluttering—has attracted an equally large and devoted following.

Don has made more than 6,000 public appearances on behalf of cleaning and decluttering, including TV, radio, and his popular in-person speeches and seminars. Don is a hands-on, high-energy worker who lives and breathes the idea that "*Clean* is the most liberating word in the English language." He also has the world's largest cleaning museum and cleaning library, and is a consultant for companies across the country on cleaning and maintenance.

He and his wife Barbara have six children and eighteen grandchildren, and divide their time between their ranch in southern Idaho and their winter home in Kauai, Hawaii.

Your Success Report

Now's your chance to tell your story—be the office dejunker of the year! How did you do it? Share your experiences by sending your report to me at the following address or by e-mail to *don@aslett.com:*

Don Aslett
PO Box 700-O
Pocatello, ID 83204

- How much junk did you have?
- How long did it take you to dejunk?
- Did you do it all at once, or in installments?
- What was the hardest thing about it/were the worst problem areas?
- Was any part of it easier than you expected?
- What did you find the hardest to part with?
- How did you manage to do it?
- What was the biggest surprise to you?
- Would you mind being quoted in future books or articles on this subject?

Dear Don:

Please put my name and the following friends of mine on your mailing list for the **Clean Report** bulletin and catalog:

Name _____

Street Address _____

City, ST Zip _____

Name _____

Street Address _____

City, ST Zip _____

Name _____

Street Address _____

City, ST Zip _____

Name _____

Street Address _____

City, ST Zip _____

Index